Edmund Fry

Pantographia

Containing accurate copies of all the known alphabets in the world

Edmund Fry

Pantographia
Containing accurate copies of all the known alphabets in the world

ISBN/EAN: 9783744715256

Printed in Europe, USA, Canada, Australia, Japan

Cover: Foto ©Paul-Georg Meister /pixelio.de

More available books at **www.hansebooks.com**

PANTOGRAPHIA;

CONTAINING

ACCURATE COPIES OF ALL THE KNOWN ALPHABETS IN THE WORLD;

TOGETHER WITH

AN ENGLISH EXPLANATION OF THE PECULIAR FORCE OR POWER OF EACH LETTER:

TO WHICH ARE ADDED,

SPECIMENS OF ALL WELL-AUTHENTICATED

ORAL LANGUAGES;

FORMING

A COMPREHENSIVE DIGEST OF

PHONOLOGY.

By EDMUND FRY,

LETTER-FOUNDER, TYPE-STREET.

Printed by COOPER and WILSON,

For JOHN and ARTHUR ARCH, Gracechurch-Street; JOHN WHITE, Fleet-Street; JOHN EDWARDS, Pall-Mall; and JOHN DEBRETT, Piccadilly.

MDCCXCIX.

1799

TO

Sir JOSEPH BANKS, Bart. K. B.

PRESIDENT OF THE ROYAL SOCIETY, &c.

Whose Patronage and Encouragement

Are liberally extended to the Promotion of

All the

Useful and ornamental Arts;

With his Permission,

THIS WORK

Is respectfully inscribed,

by

The AUTHOR

ERRATA.

PREFACE, page xvii, line 18—For *impression*, read *imperfection*.
Page 31, line 4—For *Chap.* 4, read *Chap.* 3.
Page 41, line 5—For *version*, read *reading*.
Page 121, line 10—For *antiquarians*, read *antiquaries*.
Page 173, line 35—For *their*, read *it's*; and for *were*, read *was*.
Page 191, line 6—For *five being simple*, read *five simple*.
Page 237, line 14—For *Political*, read *Philosophical*.

PREFACE.

WE cannot expect that all our Readers will be unanimous in their opinions respecting a Work of such novelty, variety, and extent, as this: some may notice redundancies, or omissions; others, we fear, will find deficiencies and imperfections: for some of these, we shall make the best apology in our power. There is one point, however, on which, we believe, there will be no diversity of opinion—the importance of the subject.—The noblest acquisition of mankind is speech; and the most useful art is that of rendering it visible: *that* distinguishes Man from the brute creation; *this* raises him to a pre-eminence above the savages of his own species.

The uses of legible language are too various to be enumerated. By the wonderful invention of writing, we are enabled to record and perpetuate our thoughts for our own benefit, or give them the most extensive communication for that of others. Without this art, the labors of our ancestors, in every branch of knowledge, would have been lost to us; tradition being so nearly allied to fable, that no authentic history can be compiled but from written materials.—From this source, and from ancient paintings, sculptures, and medals, have philosophy, science, and the arts, derived all their successive improvements: succeeding generations have been enabled to add to the stock they received from the past, and to prepare the way for future acquisitions.

By

By this happy mode of communication, distance is, as it were, annihilated, and the merchant, scholar, and statesman, become present to every purpose of utility, in the most remote regions.

The desire of communicating ideas seems to be implanted in every human breast: the two most useful methods of gratifying this desire are, by sounds addressed to the ear, or by representations or marks exhibited to the eye; or, in other words, by *Speech*, and *Writing*. The first method was rendered more complete by the invention of the second, because it opened a door to the communication of ideas, through the sense of *sight*, as well as that of *hearing*.—Speech may be considered as the substance; and writing, as the shadow that follows it.

The art of drawing ideas into vision, or of exhibiting the conceptions of the mind, by legible characters, may justly be deemed the noblest and most beneficial invention of which human ingenuity can boast—an invention which has contributed, more than all others, to the improvement of mankind.

The incalculable advantages that Man enjoys in consequence of his possessing the privilege of *language*, and the apparent impossibility of it's being the production of human beings, has induced ancient philosophers and modern philologists, very generally, to conclude that it was originally derived from the immediate communication of the Deity.—As this is a question on which sacred history has been silent, our opinions must rest upon the probability of the thing itself.

If language consisted of simple vocal sounds, as those uttered by cattle, sheep, or new-born children; of those varied by musical tones; or of signs produced by the motions, positions, and attitudes of the human body and limbs; there would be no difficulty in ascribing it's origin to the natural progress of human beings in a state of society: but the wonderful circumstance respecting *language* is, that it consists of vocal sounds modified by Articulations. Homer and Hesiod add the epithet *articulating* to Man, as characteristic of his pre-eminence.

Some of the ancients who embraced the Atomic philosophy of Epicurus, and some moderns of high rank in the republic of letters, think *language* was the offspring of *human invention*, after men

men had lived long enough in a state of society, to perceive the insufficiency of *inarticulate cries and gestures* to express the increased variety and precision of their ideas.

It being thus evident that there is no instinctive, articulate language, it has become an inquiry of some importance, how mankind were first induced to fabricate articulate sounds, and to employ them for the purpose of communicating their thoughts. Children learn to speak by insensible imitation; and, when advanced some years in life, study foreign languages under proper instructors: but the first men had no speakers to imitate, no formed language to study: by what means they learned to articulate, becomes a question, on which, I apprehend, only two opinions can be formed. Either *language* must have been originally revealed from HEAVEN, or be the fruit of *human* industry. The greater part of Jews and Christians, and even some of the wisest Pagans, have embraced the former opinion; which seems to be supported by the authority of Moses, who represents the SUPREME BEING as teaching our first parents the *names* of animals. The latter opinion is held by Diodorus Siculus, Lucretius, Horace, and many other Greek and Roman writers, who consider *language* as one of the arts invented by Man.

In order to judge of the validity of the arguments which may be brought in support of either of these opinions, it will be proper to state what is agreed on by both parties.

First, Human beings invent, or make discoveries, either by accident, or by comparing means with their ends.

Second, Very few persons, even at this day, either know, or can describe, the exact means by which they articulate, though they have been employing them during the whole of their lives.

Third, To vary any invention, or improve upon it, is infinitely more easy, and totally different from being the author of such invention; yet we do not find any improvement, or scarcely any difference in articulation, from the days of Moses to this time: and if any person now, with every advantage in his favor, were to attempt the invention or introduction of a few *new* articulations, he would be convinced of it's extreme difficulty.

Fourth, Therefore, if *men* did invent articulations, it must have

have been by accidental discovery, and in a state of highly-improved society.

The principal arguments in favor of language being of *human* invention, may be comprised under the following heads, viz.

1. The silence of the sacred writers on the subject. But it must be observed in reply, that Moses describes our first parents as using *articulate* language, immediately after their creation.

2. As the principal argument on the other side is drawn from the *immense difficulty* of inventing articulate language, so the supporters of *human* invention appear most anxious to diminish, and even annihilate the difficulty.

They state, that vocal sounds, tones, and gestures, are sufficient to unite men in the desire of forming societies, and to enable them to join in enterprizes, interesting to the whole community; which part of the argument may be supported by the examples of the Bee and the Beaver.

When men are united in a state of improved society, and have been in habits of enterprize of common concern, the necessity of a rapid and distinct communication of ideas will make a forcible impression on them. Musical tones require a musical ear, or, at least, a power of sounding and distinguishing, in order to render them useful signs of ideas: and the difficulty of teaching speakers and hearers to understand each other distinctly by these means, is, perhaps, the reason that such sounds do not form a part of any known language.

With respect to the communication of ideas by means of signs and gestures of the body, it is obvious that they can have no place, unless the speaker and hearer (if I may be allowed the expression) have the power of seeing each other distinctly. Such a part of language is therefore useless, in the night, to the blind, or to those who are prevented from seeing each other.

These considerations would sufficiently impress the advantage and importance of a language intelligible at all speaking distances, and pave the way to the improvement of the powers of the human organs of utterance. The great difficulty appears in acquiring the *first* articulations; for when a few had been received and established, their utility and importance must have been

been so striking, that attempts to extend and diversify the little stock would not long be wanted.

Now, say the favorers of this side of the question, the hissing of the Serpent would teach us, by imitation, to articulate the S, which condensed becomes Z, and aspirated makes SH; accordingly these are three radical articulations in all languages: and the hissing of the Goose would suggest the TH and T, which lead to the dense TH in the words *this*, *there*, &c., pronounced by foreigners *dis*, *dere*, &c.; thus seven articulations might have been produced. The sudden closing of the lips, by accident or design, during the enunciation of any vocal sound, would produce P, which condensed is B or V, and are accordingly radical articulations in all languages.

Such a progress as this being made with so much ease, the argument drawn from the difficulty of the invention loses its force, and, as they infer, *nodus deo vindice dignus* vanishes.

Some authors, and those too of considerable eminence, instead of attempting to shew how men could and did accomplish so difficult a work as the formation of articulate language, content themselves with such observations as the following:—"*Vocal* "sounds are founded in nature, and man would vary those "sounds, as impelled by his passions, or urged by his necessities. "This exercise of the organs of speech would produce articulate "voices, which are peculiar to the human species; vocal sounds "expressive of emotions, being natural to brutes, as well as to "men. These *articulate* voices are the first advances towards "the formation of a language. The human organs are not, "like those of most brutes, confined to a particular species of "sound; but as men are capable of learning to imitate the "several sounds of the brute creation, by those means they ac-"quire a greater variety of sounds than other animals."

In answer, however, to this way of getting rid of the difficulty, we may observe,

1. That no nation, *however savage*, has been found destitute of sounds modified by articulation; therefore, that they were not the inventors of them; because savages are confessed, by the opposers of our opinion, to be incapable of such an invention *.

2. Sup-

* *Vide* Lord Monboddo, &c.

2. Supposing any individual in a state of improved society, such as has been represented, to have invented the manner, or rather observed the power of the human voice to articulate, how could he persuade the rest of the community to adopt so extraordinary an innovation? If proposed to them on mere human authority, would not the Elders reject it as a childiſh suggestion, which they had neither motive nor power to adopt? For we know that articulation cannot be learned after a certain age.—The inventor, if any, must have been young; and his youth would be an obstacle to his success in propagating his discovery on one hand; and the immense labor and time necessary for old people to acquire eighteen or twenty articulations, and that merely on speculation, would effectually prevent it's adoption on the other, as the importance of the invention could only be demonstrated by learning and trial.

3. If every separate colony had invented it's own articulations, inſtead of that uniformity we every where find, infinite diversity muſt have presented itself.

4. We do not admit that any imitation of animals could have taught the letters above mentioned, much less the N, M, R, F, L, the guttural CH, or Welch LL; therefore this account of the origin of articulations cannot be admitted on mere conjecture.

* Those who are of opinion that language is of divine origin, consider this account of it's being of human invention, as a series of mere suppositions, not founded on any fixed principle.

The opinions of Diodorus, Vitruvius, Horace, Lucretius, and Cicero, frequently quoted in it's support, are, in their eſtimation, of no greater authority, than those of other men: for, as language was formed, and brought to a great degree of perfection, long before the æra of any historian with whom we are acquainted, the antiquity of the Greek and Roman writers does not give them any advantage in this inquiry over modern philosophers.

Aristotle has defined Man to be ζωον μιμητικον: and the definition is certainly so far just, that Man is much more remarkable for imitation than invention; and therefore, say the reasoners on this

* Warburton, Delancy, Johnſon, Beattie, Blair, &c.

this side of the question, had the human race been originally *mutum et turpe pecus*, they would have continued so, unless they had been taught to speak by some superior intelligence.

Moses, setting aside his claim to inspiration, deserves, from the consistency of his narrative, at least as much credit as Mochus, Democritus, or Epicurus; and, from his prior antiquity, if antiquity could have any weight on this subject, he would deserve more, having lived nearer to the period of which they all write. But the question respecting the origin of language may be decided without resting on authority of any kind, but merely by considering the nature of speech, and the mental and corporeal powers of Man.

Those who maintain it to be of human invention, suppose men, at first, to have been solitary animals, and afterwards to have associated without government or subordination; then to have formed political bodies, and, by their own exertions, to have advanced from the grossest ignorance to the refinements of science. But, say the reasoners, whose cause we espouse, this is a supposition contrary to all history or experience: there is not on record a well-authenticated instance, of a people emerging, by their own efforts, from barbarism to civilization. There have, indeed, been many nations raised from the state of savages; but it is known that they were polished by the influence of individuals or colonies from nations more enlightened than themselves.

The original savages of Greece were tamed by the Pelasgi, a foreign tribe; and were afterwards further polished by Orpheus, Cecrops, Cadmus, &c. who derived their knowledge from Egypt and the East. The ancient Romans, a ferocious and motley crew, received the blessings of law and religion from a succession of foreign kings; and the conquests of the Romans, at later periods, contributed to civilize the rest of Europe. In America, the only two nations which, at the invasion of the Spaniards, could be said to have advanced a single step from barbarism, were indebted for their superiority over the other tribes, not to the gradual and unassisted progress of the human mind, but to the wise institutions of foreign legislators.*

It

* *Vide* Robertson's History of America.

It is said, that before language could have been invented, mankind must have existed for ages in large political societies, and have united in some common work: but, if inarticulate cries, and the natural visible signs of the passions and affections, were modes of communication sufficiently accurate to keep a large society together for ages, and to direct it's members in the execution of some common work, what could be their inducement to the invention of an art so useless and difficult as that of articulate language? Let us, however, suppose, that different nations of savages set about to invent an art of communicating their thoughts, which, no experience could have taught them, was absolutely necessary; how came they all, without exception, to think of the one art of articulating the voice for this purpose? Inarticulate cries, out of which language is fabricated, have an instinctive connection with our passions and affections; but there are gestures, and expressions of countenance, with which our passions and affections are not in the same manner connected.

If the natural cries of passion could be so modified and enlarged as to be capable of communicating to the hearer every idea in the mind of the speaker, it is certain that the natural gestures could be so modified as to answer the very same purpose; and it is strange, that among the several nations who invented languages, not one should have attempted visible signs of their ideas, but that all should have agreed to express them by *articulated* sounds.

Every nation, whose language is narrow and rude, supplies its defects by violent gesticulations; wherefore, as much less genius is exerted in the improvement of any art than was requisite for it's first invention, it is natural to suppose, that had men been left to devise for themselves a method of communicating their thoughts, they would not have attempted any other than that by which they now improve the language transmitted by their ancestors. It is vain to urge that articulate sounds are fitter for the purpose of communicating thought than visible gesticulation: for though this may be true, it is a truth which could scarcely occur to savages, who had never experienced the fitness of either; and if, to counterbalance the superior fitness of articulation,

culation, it's extreme difficulty be taken into view, it must appear little less than miraculous, that every savage tribe should think of it rather than the easier method of artificial gesticulation.— Savages, it is well known, are remarkable for their indolence, and their preferring ease to utility; but their modes of life give such a pliancy to their bodies, that they could, with very little trouble, bend their limbs and members into any position agreed upon as the signs of ideas.

This is so far from being the case with respect to the organs of articulation, that it is with extreme difficulty, if at all, that a man, advanced in life, can be taught to articulate sounds he has not been accustomed to hear. Foreigners coming to this country after the age of thirty, seldom pronounce the language tolerably well; an Englishman at that age can hardly be taught to utter the guttural sound which the Welchman gives to the Greek χ; or even the French sound of the vowel U: and of the solitary savages who have been caught in different forests, we know not that there has been one who, after the age of manhood, learned to articulate any language so as to be readily understood.

The present age has, indeed, furnished many instances of deaf persons, while young, being taught to speak intelligibly, by skilful masters moulding the organs of the mouth into the positions proper for articulating the voice; * but who was to perform this task among the inventors of language, when all mankind were equally ignorant of the means by which articulation is effected? In a word, daily experience informs us, that men who have not learned to articulate in their childhood, never afterwards acquire the faculty of speech but by such helps as savages cannot obtain; therefore, if speech was invented at all, it must have been either by children who were incapable of invention, or by men who were incapable of speech.

A thou-

* In the Grange-road, Bermondsey, there has been establiſhed, several years, an asylum for the deaf and dumb; the beneficial effects of which are so obvious, that several children have already been discharged capable of understanding what they read or see, and of expressing all their wants by articulate language, and are now filling important stations in society.

A thousand, nay, a million of children, could not think of inventing a language. While the organs are pliable, there is not understanding enough to frame the conception of a language; and by the time that there is understanding, the organs are become too stiff for the task. Therefore, say the advocates for the divine origin of language, reason, as well as history, intimates, that mankind, in all ages, must have been speaking animals; the young having constantly acquired this art by imitating those who were older: and we may warrantably conclude, that our first parents received it by divine inspiration.

To this account of the origin of language it may be objected—If the first language was communicated by inspiration, it must have been perfect, and held in reverence by all mankind: but a vast variety of languages have prevailed in the world; and some of those which are now known, are very imperfect; and there is reason to believe that many are lost. If different languages were invented by different nations, all this would naturally follow from the mixture of these nations: but what could induce men possessed of one perfect language of divine original, to forsake it for barbarous jargons of their own invention, and in every respect inferior to that with which their forefathers or themselves had been inspired?

In answer to this objection, we urge, that nothing was given by inspiration but the faculty of speech, and the elements of language: for when once men had language, it is easy to conceive how they might have modified it by their natural powers, as thousands might improve what they could not have invented. The first language, if given by inspiration, must in its principles have had all the perfection of which language is susceptible; but, from the nature of things, it could not be very copious.

The words of language are either proper names, or the signs of ideas and relations; but it cannot be supposed that the All-wise Instructor would load the memories of men with words to denote things then unknown, or with the signs of ideas which they had not then acquired. It was sufficient that a foundation was laid, of such a nature as would support the largest superstructure which they might ever after have occasion to raise upon it; and that they were taught the method of building it by by composition and derivation. This would long preserve the language radically the same, though it could not prevent the introduction of different dialects into the different countries over which men might spread themselves.

In whatever region we may suppose the human race to have been originally placed, the increase of their numbers would, in process of time, either disperse them into various nations, or extend the one nation to a vast distance on every side. In either case, they would every where meet with new objects, which would occasion the invention of new names; and as the difference of climate, and other natural causes, would compel those who moved eastward or northward to adopt manners, in many respects, different from the modes of those who settled in the west and south, a vast number of words would in one country be fabricated, to denote complex conceptions, which must of course be unintelligible to the body of the people inhabiting countries where those conceptions could never be formed: thus would various dialects be unavoidably introduced into the original language, even whilst all mankind continued in one society, and under one government. But after separate and independent societies were formed, these variations would become more numerous, and the several dialects would deviate farther and farther from each other, as well as from the idiom and genius of the parent tongue, in proportion to the diversity of manners of the tribes by whom they were spoken. If we suppose a few persons to have been banished together from the society of their brethren, or to have wandered of their own accord to a distance, from which, through trackless forests, or other causes, they could not return, it is easy to see how the most copious language must soon have become narrow, and how the offspring of inspiration must in time have become so deformed, as scarcely to retain a feature of the ancestor whence it originally sprang.

Men do not long retain a practical skill in those arts which they never exercise: and there is an abundance of facts to prove, that a single man cast upon a desart island, and having to provide the necessaries of life by his own ingenuity, would soon lose the art of speaking his mother-tongue with fluency. A small number of persons cast away together, would be likely to retain the art somewhat longer; but in a space of time, not very long, it would in a great measure be lost by them, or their posterity: in this state of banishment, as their time would be almost wholly occupied by hunting, fishing, and other means within their reach, to support a miserable existence, they would have little leisure, and perhaps less desire, to preserve by conversation the remembrance of that ease, and those comforts, of which they would now find themselves for ever deprived; and, of course, they would soon forget all the words which, in their native language, had been used to denote the accommodations and elegancies of polished life. This, at least, seems to be certain, that they would not attempt to teach their children a part of language, which in their circumstances could be of no use to them, and of which it would be impossible to make them comprehend the meaning; for where there are no ideas, the signs of them cannot be made intelligible.

From such colonies as these dispersed over the earth, it is probable that all the nations of savages have sprung; which has induced many philosophers to imagine, that the state of the savage was originally that of man: if so, we see, that from the language of inspiration a number of different dialects must unavoidably have arisen, all very rude and narrow, retaining nothing of the parent tongue, except, perhaps, the names of the most conspicuous objects in nature, and of those wants and enjoyments inseparable from humanity.

Habits of solitude dispose a savage to speak rarely; and when he does, he uses the same terms to denote different ideas: Speech, therefore, in this rude condition of men, must be extremely narrow, and very imperfect. Every region or climate suggests a different train of ideas, and creates various wants, which must be expressed either by terms entirely new, or by old ones used in a new signification. Hence must originate great diversity, even in the first elements of speech, among all savage nations; the words retained of the original language being used in various senses, and pronounced, as we may believe, with various accents. When any of those savage tribes emerged from their barbarism, whether by their own efforts, or by the aid of people more enlightened than themselves,

selves, it is obvious that the improvement and copiousness of their language would keep pace with their own progress in knowledge, and in the arts of civil life; but in the infinite multitude of words which civilization and refinement add to language, it would be little less than miraculous were any two nations to agree upon the same sounds to represent the same ideas. Superior refinement, indeed, may induce imitation, conquest may impose a language, and extension of empire may melt down different nations and dialects into one mass: but independent tribes naturally give rise to diversity of tongues; nor does it seem possible that they should retain more of the original language than the words expressive of those objects with which men are at all times equally concerned.

The variety of tongues therefore, the copiousness of some, and the narrowness of others, furnish no good objection to the divine origin of language; for whether language was at first revealed from Heaven, or in a course of ages invented by men, a multitude of dialects would inevitably arise, as soon as the human race was separated into a number of distinct and independent nations. We do not pretend to decide for our readers in a question of this nature, but have given the best arguments on both sides which we could either devise or find in the writings of others; and if it be seen, as we doubt not it will, that our own judgment leans to the side of revelation, let us not be hastily condemned by those, whose knowledge of languages extends no farther than to Greece and Rome, France and England; for if they carry their philological inquiries to the East, they may, perhaps, be able to trace the remains of one original language through a great part of the Globe at present.

Whatever opinions we adopt with respect to the origin of the first language, or the causes of the great diversity in various tongues at this day, we shall doubtless entertain the sentiment, that languages must have preceded, by many centuries, any attempt to depict the ideas of them, or to denote the sounds by permanently visible marks. It is only in a highly-cultivated state of society that written language can be necessary. The first attempts to depict thought, would undoubtedly be rude and imperfect

imperfect representations of visible objects; such as were found among the Mexicans on the discovery of America.

A *lion* might be sketched to import fierceness or valour; an *ox*, to denote strength; a *stag*, swiftness; and a *hare*, to intimate timidity, &c.

The next step in this process would naturally extend to the inventing and appropriating of a few arbitrary characters for representing abstract and other ideas, which could not be well ascertained by the methods above mentioned; which arbitrary signs might readily acquire a currency by compact, as money and medals do over a great part of the world: upon this plan, we imagine, the ancient Chinese formed their manner of writing their language.

But neither the picture nor the hieroglyphic, nor the method of denoting ideas by arbitrary characters appropriated by compact, could ever have arrived at such perfection, as to answer all the purposes of ideal communication. The grand desideratum then would be, to fabricate characters to represent simple sounds, and to reduce these characters to so small a nnmber as to be easily learned and preserved in the memory. In this attempt the Chinese have notoriously failed: their letters, or rather their characters, being so numerous, that few, if any, of their most industrious scholars, have been able to learn and retain the whole catalogue: indeed those people are not able to conceive how any combinations of twenty or thirty characters should be competent to all the purposes of written language.

There is little difficulty in conceiving a gradual abridgement, or contraction of these pictures, till we arrive at the state in which the Chinese alphabet (if we may use such an expression) is found at present; but we cannot suppose that a people who had arrived at such a degree of perfection in expressing their ideas by visible signs, should ever discover a gradual method of passing over to the use of alphabets, or suddenly abandon their inveterate habits at the instigation of any individual, who may have discovered the superior excellency of that manner of denoting language.

These considerations lead us to inquire, whether it is probable that men, in any state of society, could have invented and introduced

introduced among their fellow-citizens the use of an alphabet, without supernatural assistance; or whether it is probable that any progressive improvement of the human mind, could change symbolic or picture writing into that of alphabetical characters.

That alphabets, as well as language, are of divine origin, is attempted to be supported by the following considerations, viz.

Much has been written, and numerous hypotheses proposed, to investigate the origin of alphabetic writing; to give even an abridged account of which, would far exceed the limits of this Preface.

Many nations have claimed the honour of this invention. The Greeks ascribed it to the Phenicians, and consequently used the word φοινικιζειν, to *act the Phenician*, in the same sense with αναγινωσκειν, *to read*: and Lucan ascribes the invention to the same ingenious people.

That the Assyrian, Chaldaic, and Hebrew languages, were the same, most of the learned are fixed in their opinions; and that their alphabets are of antidiluvian antiquity, appears highly probable: for had an invention of such vast importance to mankind been made since that period, we conclude the author would have been commemorated in the annals of the country in which he lived. Josephus, book 1, chap. 3, informs us, that Seth erected two pillars, one of brick, and the other of stone, and inscribed upon them their astronomical observations, and other improvements, (See Chaldean, No. 4, page 31, of this work); which shews that there did exist such an opinion of the antiquity of the art of writing.

Among the European nations we do not find any who pretend to the invention of letters. All of them derived the art from the Romans, except the Turks, who had it from the Arabians. The Romans never claimed the discovery, but confessed their knowledge to have been received from the Greeks, who owned that they had it from the Phenicians, who, as well as their colonists the Carthaginians, spoke a dialect of the Hebrew scarcely varying from the original. The Coptic resembles the Greek in most of its characters, and is therefore referred to the same original. The Chaldean, Syriac, and latter Samaritan, are dialects

dialects of the Hebrew, without any considerable deviation, or many additional words.

The Ethiopic differs more from the Hebrew, but less from the Arabic; all these languages have issued from the same stock, as the similarity of their formation, and the numberless words common to them all, sufficiently evince. Alterations would naturally be produced, in proportion to the civilization of the several nations, and their intercourse with others, which will account for the superior copiousness of some above the rest. It appears then, that all the languages in use among men that have been conveyed in alphabetical characters, have been those of people connected ultimately or immediately with the Hebrews, to whom we are indebted for the earliest specimens of the communication of ideas by writing.

This proposition will be farther confirmed, by considering the sameness of the artificial denominations of the letters in the Oriental, Greek and Latin languages, accompanied by a similar arrangement, as *alpha*, *beta*, &c. It may still be objected, however, that the characters employed by the ancients to discriminate their letters, are entirely dissimilar: it may be urged, why should not one nation adopt from another the mode of expressing the art, as well as the art itself? Such an effect would not be very likely to take place, before the art of printing had established an uniformity of character.

The old Samaritan is precisely the same as the Hebrew language; and the Samaritan Pentateuch does not vary a single letter in twenty words from the Hebrew: but the characters are very different; for the Jews adopted the Chaldaic letters during their captivity at Babylon, instead of those of their forefathers.

What we know of those nations who have continued for many centuries unconnected with the rest of the world, strongly militates against the hypothesis of the human invention of alphabetical writing. The experiment has been fairly made upon the ingenuity of mankind, both Chinese and savage, for a longer period than that which is supposed to have produced alphabetic writing by regular gradations, which decidedly concludes against this art being of human invention.

The

The Chinese, a people famous for their discoveries and mechanical genius, have made some advances towards the delineation of their ideas, by arbitrary signs; nevertheless, have been unable to accomplish this exquisite device; and, after so long a trial to no purpose, we may reasonably infer, that their mode of writing, which is growing more intricate and voluminous every day, will never terminate in so clear, so comparatively simple, an expedient, as that of alphabetical characters.

We shall consider the argument on which the commonly received supposition entirely depends; that is, the natural gradation through the several species of symbols acknowledged to have been in use with various people, terminating by an easy transition, in the detection of alphabetical characters: we believe the strength of this argument will be fairly appreciated from the following representation.

The first method of embodying ideas would be by drawing a representation of the images themselves: the impression of which method is very obvious, both on account of it's tediousness, and inability to go beyond external appearances, or to denote the abstract ideas of the mind.

The next method would be somewhat more general, and would substitute two or three circumstances for the whole transaction: so two Kings, for example, engaging each other with military weapons, might convey the idea of a war between two nations. This abbreviated method would be more expeditious than the former; but what is gained in conciseness would be lost in perspicuity. It is a description more compendious indeed, but still a description of outward objects alone; to which head may be referred the picture-writing of the Mexicans.

The next advance would be to the use of symbols—the incorporation, as it were, of abstract and complex ideas in figurer, more or less generalized in proportion to the improvement of it. Thus, in the earlier stages of this device, a circle might express the sun, or a semicircle the moon, which is only a contraction of the foregoing method. This symbol-writing, in it's advanced state, would become more refined, but enigmatical and mysterious in proportion to that refinement: hence it would be less

fit

fit for common use—therefore more particularly appropriate to philosophy and religion.

This method being still too subtile and complicated for general use, the only plan to be pursued was a reduction of the first stage of the preceeding; thus a dot instead of a circle might stand for the sun, and a similar abbreviation might be extended to all the symbols. On this scheme, every object and idea would have it's appropriate mark, which might be multiplied in proportion to the works of nature and the operations of the mind. This plan was also practised by the Egyptians, but has been carried to greater perfection by the Chinese; the vocabulary of the latter is therefore capable of being extended to any imaginary length. But if we compare this tedious and awkward contrivance with the astonishing brevity and perspicuity of alphabetical writing, we must be persuaded that no two things can be more dissimilar; and that the transition from a scheme constantly enlarging itself, and growing daily more intricate, to the expression of every possible idea by a modified arrangement of twenty-four marks, is not so very easy and perceptible as may be imagined: indeed, this seems still to be rather an expression of things, in a manner similar to the second stage of symbol-writing, than the notification of ideas by arbitrary signs.

To all this we shall subjoin the following remarks, to give strength to the foregoing reasoning, viz.

1st, Pliny asserts the use of letters to have been eternal; which shews the antiquity of the practice to have extended beyond the era of authentic history.

2d, The cabalistic doctors of the Jews maintain, that alphabetic writing was one of the ten things which God created on the evening of the sabbath.

3d, Most of the profane authors of antiquity ascribe the use of alphabetical characters to the Egyptians, who, according to some, received them from Mercury; or, as others suppose, from their god Teuth.

These are mere conjectures and fables.

Many pious and learned authors have contended, that the alphabet was first given with the law from Mount Sinai; but we presume

presume the following state of facts will invalidate such an opinion.

The first mention of *Writing* recorded in Scripture, will be found in Exod. xvii. 14. "*And the* LORD *said unto* Moses, *Write* "*this for a memorial, in a book; and rehearse it in the ears of* " Joshua; *for I will utterly put out the remembrance of* Amalek "*from under Heaven.*" This command was given immediately after the defeat of the Amalekites near Horeb, and before the arrival of the Israelites at Mount Sinai.

It is observable that there is not the least hint to induce us to believe that writing was then newly invented; on the contrary, we may conclude that Moses understood what was meant by *writing in a book*; otherwise the ALMIGHTY would have instructed him, as he did Noah in building the ark; for he would not have commanded him to *write* in a book, if he had been ignorant of the art of writing: but Moses did not express any difficulty of comprehension when he received this command.— We also find, that Moses wrote all the words, and all the judgements of the LORD, contained in the 21st and two following chapters of Exodus, before the two written tables of stone were so much as *promised*. The delivery of the tables is not mentioned till the 18th verse of the 31st chapter, after GOD had made an end of communing with him on the Mount, though the ten commandments were promulgated immediately after his third descent.

It is also observable, that Moses no where mentions that the alphabet was a *new thing* in his time, much less that he was the inventor of it; on the contrary, he speaks of the art of writing, as a thing well known, and in familiar use; for Exod. xxviii. 21, he says, "And the stones shall be with the names of the chil- " dren of Israel, *Twelve*; according to their names, *like the* "*engravings of a signet*, every one with his name, shall they be, " according to the *twelve* tribes." And again, v. 36, "And " thou shalt make a plate of pure gold, and *grave* upon it, *like* " the engravings of a signet, HOLINESS TO THE LORD."— Can language be more expressive? Would it not be absurd to deny, that this sentence must have been in *words* and *letters?* But writing was known and practised by the people in general,

in

in the time of Moses, as appears from the following texts, Deut. vi. 9, xi. 20, xvii. 18, xxiv. 1, xxvii. 3, 8. By the last text the *people* were commanded to *write* the law on stones; and it is to be noticed, that some of the above texts relate to transactions *previous* to the delivery of the law at Mount Sinai.

If we call the different dialects of the various nations that inhabit the known parts of the Globe, languages, the number is truly great; and vain and useless would be his ambition who should attempt to learn them. We shall begin with naming the principal, which are four, and may be termed the original or mother-tongues, and seem to have given birth to all that are spoken in Europe, *viz.* the Latin, Celtic, Gothic and Sclavonian. It will not, however, be imagined, from the term *original* given to these languages, that we believe them to have been handed to us without any alteration, from the confusion of tongues at the building of the tower of Babel. We have expressed our opinion, that there was but one truly original language, from which all others are derivations variously modified. The four tongues just mentioned are original only, as being the immediate parents of those now spoken in Europe.

From the Latin came

The Italian, Spanish, Portuguese, and French; and

From the Celtic,

The Welch, Erse or Gaelic, Irish, Bretagne or Aremorican, and that of the Waldenses.

From the Gothic,

The High and Low Dutch; the English, which is also enriched with the spoils of many other languages; the Danish, Norwegian, Swedish, and the Icelandic or Runic.

From the Sclavonian,

The Polish, Lithuanian, Bohemian, Vandalian, Croatian, Russian, Carnish, Dalmatian, Lusatian, Moldavian, and many others.

The languages at present generally spoken in Asia are,

The Turkish, Tartarian, Persian and modern Arabic, Georgian, Armenian, modern Indian, Formosan, Indosanic, Tamoulic or Malabaric, the Chinese, Japonese, &c.

Here we have enumerated only such Asiatic languages, of which

which we have some knowledge by alphabets, grammars, or other books; there are, doubtless, many other tongues and dialects in those vast regions and adjacent islands, of which we are not able to give any account.

The principal languages of Africa are,

The Egyptian, Fetuitic, or of the kingdom of Fetu, the Mauritanian or Moroccan, and the jargon of those savage nations inhabiting the deserts.—The people on the coast of Barbary speak a corrupt dialect of the Arabic: to these may be added the Chilhic, or Tamazeght, the Negritian, and that of Guinea, the Abyssinian, and that of the Hottentots.

The languages of the American nations are but little known in Europe. Those of the Mexicans and Peruvians seem to be the most regular and polished; there is also one, called Poconchi, used in the bay of Honduras, the words and rules of which are known to us. The languages of North America are, in general, the Algonhic, the Apalachian, Mohawk, and those of Savannah, Virginia, and Mexico. In South America, the Peruvian, the Caribic, the Cairic, and the Tucumanian, with the languages of Chili, Paraguay, Brasil, and Guiana. But there can be no doubt that in North America the English and French, and in South America the Spanish languages, prevail more extensively than any others.

Having already observed that it would be a vain undertaking for any man to attempt the study of all these languages, and to make his head an universal dictionary; so it would be absurd in us to offer any analysis of them in this place: but a few reflections may, perhaps, be permitted.

Among the modern languages of Europe, the French deserves great attention: it is elegant and pleasing; and is therefore become so general, that with it we may make the tour of this quarter of the globe without much need of an interpreter.

The German and Italian likewise merit particular notice; as does the English, perhaps above all, for it's many and great excellencies.—See p. 60 of this work.

The other languages of Europe have their beauties and excellencies; but the greatest difficulty in all living languages is in the pronunciation, which is scarcely possible for any one to attain,

attain, unless he were born or educated in the country where it is spoken: and it is very difficult to extend our knowledge so far as to be able to form a critical judgment of them.

Those that are derived from the Latin have the advantage of adopting, without restraint, and without offending the ear, Greek and Latin words and expressions; which privilege is forbidden the Germans, who, in their best compositions, dare not use any foreign word, unless it be some technical term in case of great necessity.

Such is the general sketch of the origin and diffusion of languages and alphabets, which we apprehend will be deemed sufficient to shew the extent and importance of the subject. We shall now proceed with some account of the execution of the work.

The design of this work is to promote the diffusion of Science, which is effected in all cases, by facilitating the communication of ideas, at present done by means of oral or written language only.

The limits prescribed to this Volume render it impossible for the Author to enter into minute details or anecdotes, even of the most important languages: his view is rather to give an outline of the subject, to shew what is commonly known, and to put it into the power of philologists to extend the sphere of our knowledge; and to furnish them with a centre of communication, to which their researches and discoveries may be directed. He has, therefore, only given what he promised; hoping it will enable both his friends and critics to state the errors, omissions, redundancies, &c. which he will endeavour to rectify on some future occasion. No extensive work was ever brought to perfection at once; but something must be begun to form a ground for criticism and improvement.

Secret alphabets, or methods of conducting private correspondences, admit of infinite diversity; and as no one method has ever obtained generally in any country, they were not judged admissible in a work of this kind. The only, or, at least, most impenetrable method of secret correspondence, is by means of the same edition of a printed or manuscript book, possessed by each correspondent; so that the word intended may be found, by quoting the page, line, and word of that line,

which

which may be conducted in such a manner as to frustrate all the principles of decyphering.

The note respecting each alphabet or specimen contains the time when it was used; the inventor or patron; the time it continued in use or flourished; and the authorities for these several circumstances, as far as could be collected.

We cannot vouch for the authenticity of the ancient alphabets, as those of Adam, Noah, Ninus, &c.; but in a work professing to exhibit all, it was thought proper to give those met with on respectable authority.

There is no doubt that all the alphabets in the world are very imperfect, in point of letters, for the several simple or usual sounds in those languages; as, perhaps, no tongue can express it's words with less than about forty characters.

For the reason above alleged, we have not attempted to give short hand, or secret alphabets, the most approved systems of which are Holdsworth and Aldridge, Gurney, Hodgson, Blanchard and Byrom.

The principal object of an undertaking of this nature is to exhibit correct copies or representations of those alphabets which are at present known: for this purpose, the Author has spared no pains nor expense in procuring the most authentic originals and engraved copies which have come to his knowledge. He cannot omit this opportunity of expressing his grateful acknowledgments to those liberal and enlightened Antiquaries who have so kindly communicated their stores with him. From these sources he has copied every character with his own hand, and with all the exactness in his power.

With respect to the sound or force of each letter, the Author has collected them from the same respectable authorities; but it will be obvious to his learned readers, that no combination of letters in one language, can exactly represent the pronunciation of those of another: for instance, no letters in the English can represent the sound of the French *u*, *eu*, *en*, &c. If the Author could not, in the compass allotted to this work, enter into a discussion of the pronunciation of the letters of the several alphabets, still less would it have been consistent with his plan, had he been qualified for the task, to enter upon the grammatical construction or peculiarities of the different languages.—

Though

Though oral languages are not strictly connected with an exhibition of alphabets, yet the Author concluded that it would be a considerable gratification to his readers to see the diversity of dialects which have arisen from the original tongue, if any such existed.

The alphabetical arrangement of the matter of this work has been preferred to any other mode with an index, and we trust it will be generally most approved; but great care has been taken to place alphabets, or languages of one name, in chronological order.

Many alphabets and dialects having received a variety of names, all of which could not, with propriety, be introduced under the alphabetic titles, a Table of Synonymes is added, to facilitate the finding of any article: which Table the reader is referred to, if he find himself at any loss in this respect: for example, *Sanskrita* is not found in the alphabetical arrangement, but under the more appropriate name *Nagari*, &c.

We have given a list of those Subscribers who have favoured us with permission to insert their names; and feel grateful for this public testimony of their approbation of the undertaking. The support of so many known friends to Literature and the Arts, has animated the Author to exertions which he could not have made on the suggestions of his own solitary opinion. His warmest acknowledgments are also due to those Gentlemen, distinguished by their learning and science in antiquities, by whose assistance he has added to the collection upwards of seventy articles since the publication of the Prospectus. If his feeble endeavours may be hereafter found to have been in any degree of service to the Literary World, and a future amended edition of, or a supplement to, the Pantographia, may meet encouragement, as the Plan is now before the Public; he will solicit the kind assistance of the Antiquary, the Virtuoso, and of every Gentleman possessed of an alphabet, or specimen of oral language, of good authority, which shall be faithfully given in the work. He is sensible that, in a work of this kind, the candid Critic may find many opportunities for the display of his learning and acumen; but he hopes the novelty, extent, and importance of the subject, will shield his errors or omissions from the severity of censure.

TABLE

TABLE of SYNONYMES.

For Belgic, ...	*See*	Low Dutch.
Bramin, ...		Nagari.
Bretagne, ...		Aremorican.
Chancery text, . . .		English 16.
Church text, . . .		Ditto 20.
Court or Exchequer, .		Ditto 18.
Damot Agow, . . .		Ethiopic 1.
Erse, ...		Celtic.
Etrurian, . . .		Etruscan.
Engrossing or Secretary,		English 21.
Falasha, ...		Ethiopic 1.
Gaelic, ...		Celtic.
Gafat, ...		Ethiopic 1.
Galla, ...		Ditto.
Geez, ...		Ditto.
Hibernian, ...		Irish.
Iberian, ...		Georgian.
Kufic, ...		Arabic 1.
Moroccan, ...		Ditto 4.
Pali, ...		Bali.
Papuan, ...		New Guinea.
Pelasgic, ...		Greek 1, 2, and 3.
Rhætian, ...		Grisons.
Sanskrita, ...		Nagari.
Swiss, ...		Helvetian.
Tcheratz Agow, . . .		Ethiopic 1.
Tuſcan, ...		Etruscan.

☞ Under Samaritan, Hebrew, Chaldean, Greek, Latin, &c. will be found several varieties of character, distinguished by particular names, which were not thought necessary to be enumerated in this place.

AUTHO-

AUTHORITIES *quoted in this Work.*

Oratio Dominica, plus centum *linguis*, *Versionibus*, aut *Characteribus* reddita et expressa. 4to. Lond. 1713.

Oratio Dominica, in diversas ominum fere Gentium linguas versa, et propriis cujusque linguæ characteribus expressa. Editore Johanne Chamberlaynio. 4to. Amst. 1715.

Dr. Barnard's Tables. Oxford, 1689.

Dr. Morton's Tables. London, 1759.

Manuel Typographique. Par Fournier le Jeune, 2 vols, 12mo. Paris, 1766.

Essay towards a real Character, and Philosophical Language, by John Wilkins, D. D. folio, London, 1668.

Encyclopedie Françoise, folio, Livourne, 1772.

Thresor de l'Histoire des Langues de cest Univers. Par M. Claude Duret. 4to. Yverdon, 1619.

An Analysis of the Galic Language, by William Shaw, A. M. 12mo. Edinb. 1778.

Unheard-of Curiosities concerning the talismanical Sculpture of the Persians, &c. by James Gaffarel, 12mo. Lond. 1650.

Ezechielis Spanhemii dissertationes de usu et præstantia numismatum antiquorum, folio, 1704.

Recherches Nouvelles sur la Science des Medailles, &c. par Poinsinet de Sivry, 4to. Mæstricht, 1778.

Rerum Sicularum Scriptores præcipui ex recentioribus, &c. Auctor Thomas Fazellus, folio, Francofurti ad Mœnum, 1579.

History of the Origin and Progress of Printing, by Philip Luckombe, 8vo. London, 1774.

A new

A new System of modern Geography, by W. Guthrie, Esq. 4to. London, 1795.

Dictionary of the English Language, by Samuel Johnson, L.L.D. 2 vols. 4to. London, 1785.

Chronicon Saxonicum, ex MSS. codicibus, &c. by Edmund Gibson, A.B. 4to. Oxford, 1692.

Institutions of Language, containing a Physico-grammatical Essay on the propriety and rationale of the English Tongue, by B. Martin, 8vo. London, 1748.

On the radical Letters of the Pelasgians, and their derivatives, by Thomas Astle, Esq. F.R.S. and F.A.S. 4to. London, 1785.

The Origin and Progress of Writing, as well Hieroglyphic as Elementary, &c. &c. By Thomas Astle, Esq. F.R.S. F.A.S. &c. 4to. London, 1784.

A Voyage round the World in the years 1785, 6, 7, and 8, by J. F. G. de la Pérouse, 8vo. London, 1798.

Epreuves Generales des Characteres, avec un traité des Langues Etrangeres, de leurs Alphabets, et des Chiffres. A LA PLUME. Par le Clabart, folio, Paris.

This is an extraordinary specimen of hand-writing in imitation of every kind of printing and wood cuts, on 651 pages of vellum; it also contains specimens from 58 books, independent of those which are complete, viz. La Nef des Fous du Monde—La Danse Macabre—La Danse de Mort, en Allemande—Le Nom de Dieu en Cinquante Langues, &c. &c.—*The drawings are executed with wonderful spirit, and the whole forms an astonishing monument of ingenuity and patience; bound in morocco, with gilt leaves.*

This curious Unique is in the Author's possession.

The Origin and Progress of Letters, by William Massey, 8vo. London, 1763.

A compendious History of the Goths, Swedes and Vandals, &c. by Olaus Magnus, Archbishop of Upsal, &c. folio, London, 1658.

Antiquitates Asiaticæ Christianam Æram Antecedentes, &c. per Edmundum Chishull, S. T. B. folio, London, 1728.

Encyclo-

Encyclopœdia Britannica, 4to. Edinburgh, 1797.

Palæographia Græca, sive de ortu et progressu Literarum Græcarum, &c. D. Bernardo de Montfaucon, folio, Parisiis, 1708.

A Voyage to New Guinea and the Moluccas, by Capt. Thomas Forrest, 4to. London, 1780.

A Discovrse of the Orientall Tongues, by Christian Ravis, 12mo. London, 1649.

Travels in Europe, Asia and Africa, by Charles Peter Thunberg, M.D. &c. 8vo. London, 1796.

Van Troil's Letters on Iceland, 8vo. 1780.

An Essay on the Irish Language, by Major Vallancy, 12mo. Dublin, 1772.

Vocabularia Linguarum Totius Orbis Comparativa, collected by command of the late Empress of Russia, 2 vols. 4to. Petersburgh, 1786.

Novum Testamentum, &c. Erasmi, folio, Basil, 1570.

Biblia Sacra Castellionis, folio, Frankf. 1697.

Novum Testamentum Bezæ, folio, Genev. 1598.

Gentleman's Magazine.

Monthly Magazine.

Alphabeta Varia. Typis sacræ congregationis de propaganda fide, 2 vols. 8vo. Romæ.

Essay on Medals, by J. Pinkerton, 8vo. London, 1789.

Political, miscellaneous and philosophical Pieces, by Dr. Franklin, 8vo. London, 1779.

Remaines concerning Britain, &c. by William Camden, Esq. 4to. London, 1657.

The History of Sumatra, by William Marsden, F.R.S. 4to. London, 1783.

Linguarum duodecim characteribus differentium Alphabetum, &c. Gulielmi Postelli Diligentiâ, 4to. Paris, 1538.—*This work is not paged.*

Universal

Universal Gazetteer, by John Walker, 8vo. London, 1795.

Journal of a Voyage to the South Seas, from papers of the late Sydney Parkinson, 4to. London, 1784.

A Voyage to the Pacific Ocean, by Captains Cook, King, &c. 3 vols. 4to. London, 1785.

Antiquities of Ireland, by Edward Ledwich, L. L. B. M. R. I. A. F. A.S. 4to. Dublin, 1790.

The Antiquities, Natural History, Ruins, and other Curiosities, of Egypt, Nubia and Thebes, by Frederic Lewis Norden, 2 vols. folio, London, 1780.

Chronological Antiquities, &c. by John Jackson, 3 vols. 4to. London, 1752.

The Works of Thomas Wilson, D.D. late Bishop of Sodor and Man, 2 vols. folio, Bath, 1782.

SUBSCRIBERS.

Aynslie, Lord Charles, Littleharle Tower, Northumberland.
Adair, Alexander, Esq.
Alers, William, Esq. Fenchurch Street.
Acworth, Ball Buckridge, Esq. Marsham Street.
Allwood, Rev. P. Wandsworth.
Antrobus, Rev. P. Whitley, Cheshire.
Ashburner, Luke, Esq. Bombay.
Arch, J. and A. booksellers, 12 copies.
Ash, Gregory, Bristol.

Bute, Marquis of Bute, F. A. S.
Banks, Sir Joseph, Bart. K. B. President of the Royal Society, F. A. S. &c. &c.
Boddington, Samuel, Esq. Mark Lane.
Barnes, John, Esq. Thirlby.
Barnes, Rev. John, M. A. Master of St. Bee's School, Cumberland.
Barclay, Robert, F. L. S. Clapham Terrace.
Babington, William, M.D. Basinghall Street.
Baldwin, Henry, Esq. Bridge Street.
Bradley, Thomas, M.D. De La Hay Street, Westminster.
Brand, Rev. John, M. A. Secretary to the Society of Antiquaries.
Barry, Bartholomew, Bristol.
Bawcutt, Martin, Esq. Coventry.
Barfield, John, printer, London.
B. Rev. P. L. L. D. Deal.
Bensley, Thomas, printer, London.
Birch, Thomas, Esq.
Boys, William, Esq. F.A.S. Walmer.

Boucher,

Boucher, Rev. Jonathan, A. M. F. A. S.
Bulgin, William, Bristol.
Bishop, William, Basingstoke.
Bye, Deodatus, printer, London.
Bulmer, William, printer, London.
Bloomer, Samuel, Esq. Kingsland Crescent.
Brickwood, John, Esq. Billiter Square.

Cavendish, Henry, Esq. F.R.S. F.A.S. Trust. Brit. Mus.
Clayton, Sir Richard, Bart. Adlington, Lancashire.
Cuthbert, J. R. Esq.
Cunnington, William, Esq. Heytesbury.
Carter, Rev. J. M.A. F.A.S. head master of the Grammar school, Lincoln.
Creser, Thomas, Fenchurch Street.
Caslon, Elizabeth, Chiswell Street.
Cooper, Joseph, printer, London.
Crachrode, Rev. C. M. M.A. F.R.S. F.A.S. Trust. Brit. Mus.
Cruttwell, Richard, Bath.
Clarke, J. C. Esq. Barbican.
Capper, Jasper, Gracechurch Street.
Catley, Stephen, Esq.
Cockfield, Joseph, Upton.
Chalmers, Alex. Esq. Throgmorton Street.

Durham, Bishop of.
Disney, John, D.D. F.A.S.
Denman, Thomas, M.D.
Denman, Thomas, Esq.
Dennison, Richard, M.D. F.A.S.
Dickinson, Rev. P. A.M. Hoxton Square.
Debrett, John, bookseller, 3 copies.
Davies, John, Basingstoke.
Downes, Joseph, printer, London.
Dibdin, Charles, Esq.
Du Val, Philip, D.D. F.R.S. F.A.S.

Edwards,

Edwards, John, bookseller, 6 copies.
Ewer, Samuel, Esq.
Emery and Adams, Bristol.
Estlin, Rev. J. P. Bristol.

Frankland, William, Esq.
French, Nath. Bogle, Esq.
Fowle, William, M.D. Hungerford.
Forbes, James, Esq. Stanmore.
Ford, Thomas, Esq.
Fry, Nicholas Lacy, Esq. New Court House, Topsham.
Fry, Anna, Bristol.
Fry, Joseph Storrs, ditto.
Fry, William Storrs, Mildred's Court.
Fry, John, junior, South Street, Finsbury.
French, P. W. Reading.
Flower, B. Cambridge, 2 copies.
Fardon, William, Reading.

Garthshore, Maxwell, M.D. F.R.S. F.A.S. F.R.S. Edinb.
Galton, Samuel, F.R.S. Birmingham.
Giddy, Davies, Esq. F.R.S.
Gilpin, Joshua.
Glaister, Samuel.
Grant, Andrew, Esq. Fenchurch Street.

Henniker Major, John, Esq. M. P. F.R.S. F.A.S.
Henley, Rev. Samuel, M.A. F.A.S.
Hood, John, Esq. Newington Green.
Holloway, Thomas, ditto.
Holloway, John.
Hazard, Samuel, Bath, 6 copies.
Harford, Richard, Esq. F.A.S.
Harford, Joseph, Esq. Bristol.
Heydinger, Charles, Plumtree Street.
Hobson, William, Esq. Stamford Hill.
Holt, Daniel, printer, Newark.

Hough,

Hough, Thomas, Esq. Percy Street.
Hancock, Joseph, Basinghall Street.
Harwood, John, Esq. Dean, Hants.
How, Richard, Woburn, Bedfordshire.
Hodgkin, John, Pentonville.
Hill, John, L.L.D. University, Edinburgh.

Jermyn, George, Ipswich.
Jones, Joseph, printer, London.
Johnson, Edward, Whitechapel Road.
Juitt, George, Caddick's Row, Whitechapel.
Irton, Edmund Lamplugh, Esq. Irton Hall, Cumberland.

Kirkpatrick, Thomas, Esq. Hamburgh.
Kettle, Godfrey, Esq. Gower Street.
Knowles, George, Ely Place.
King, Thomas, junior, bookseller.

Lefevre, Charles Shaw, Esq. M.P. F.R.S. F.A.S.
Lettsom, J.C. M.D. F.R.S. F.A.S.
Lane, Edward, Esq. Basingstoke.
Lewis, William, Esq.
Lee, Captain.
Lunn, W.H. Cambridge, 6 copies.
Lee, John, Hatton Garden.
Lawson, Sir Wilfrid, Bart. Brayton, Cumberland.
Lackington, Allen and Co. 6 copies.

Marsh, Charles, Esq. F.A.S. M.R.I.A.
Marsden, William, Esq. L.L.D. F.R.S. F.A.S. M.R.I.A. M. Asiat. S.
Morton, Charles, M.D. F.R.S. F.A.S. &c.
Mason, Rev. Henry Cox, A.M. Bermondsey.
Maltby, Rev. ——, Norwich.
Marsh, Rev. T. Orlebar, F.L.S. Vicar of Stevington, Bedfordshire.

More,

More, Samuel, Esq. Adelphi.
Mainstone, James, Esq. Essex Street,
Morgan, ——, Esq. Southgate.
Martyn, Thomas.
Morton, William, Shoe Lane.
Meredith, Thomas, Crescent, Kingsland.
Mountford, Richard, Esq. Barbican.

Northumberland, Duke of, F. R.S. F.A.S.
Nichols, John, Esq. F. A. S. Edinburgh and Perth.
Noble, Richard, printer, London.
Newenham, George, Esq. Cork.

Ouseley, Major, Upper Norton Street.

Prime, Samuel, Esq. F.R.S. F.A.S.
Porson, Richard, Esq. Greek Professor, Cambridge.
Pearson, George, M. D. F.R.S.
Paynter, F. Esq. Trekenning, Cornwall.
Pole, Thomas, surgeon, Leadenhall Street.
Prichard, Thomas, Bristol.
Pine, William, ditto.
Phillips, James, George Yard.
Phillips, William, ditto.
Phillips, John, engraver.
Paas, Cornelius, Holborn,

Ray, Robert, Esq. New Court House, Topsham.
Ridout, J. G. 33, Paternoster Row.
Ring, Thomas, surgeon, Reading.
Reynolds, Deborah, Clapham.
Reynolds, Thomas, Carshalton.
Reynolds, William Foster, Clapham.
Reynolds, Jacob Foster, Carſhalton.
Rosser, Robert, Bristol,

Spencer,

Spencer, Earl, F.R.S. F.A.S. Trust. Br. Mus.
Stamford and Warrington, Earl of.
Sulivan, Rich. Jos. Esq. M.P. F.R.S. F.A.S.
Strahan, Andrew, Esq. M.P.
Society for the encouragement of Arts, Manufactures, and Commerce.
Smirnove, Rev. J. Chaplain to the Russian Ambassador.
Saunders, George, Esq.
Sims, James, M.D. Lawrence Lane.
Smith, Thomas Woodrouffe, Great Saint Helens.
Stuart, Charles, Tower Street.
Sael, George, bookseller.
Sabine, Thomas, printer.
Stephenson, Simon, Esq. Great Sanctuary,
Shipley, Richard, Esq. Horsleydown,
Sibly, Ebenezer, M.D.
Simpson, Robert, Bristol.
Stackhouse, John, Esq. F.L.S. Pendarvis, Cornwall,
Steele, Isaac, Type Street.
Skirven, John, printer, London.
Smeeton, Joseph, printer, London.
Stewart, James, perfumer, Broad Street.

Trinity College, Cambridge.
Tooke, Rev. William, F.R.S. Member of the Imperial Academy of Sciences, and of the free Economical Society at Petersburgh.
Thomason, Rev. Thomas, A.M. Cambridge.
Tomlins, T.E. Esq. Inner Temple.
Terrett, William, L.L.D. Doctor's Commons.
Thomas, W.H. surgeon, Basingstoke.
Taylor, Josiah, Architectural Library, Holborn,

Valangin, F. de, M.D. Fore Street.
Valpy, Richard, D.D, Reading.
Vansittart, N. Esq.

West,

West, Benjamin, Esq. President of the Royal Academy.
Walker, John, Esq. F.R.S. F.A.S.
Wilkins, Charles, Esq. F.R.S. M. Asiat. S.
Ware, John, printer of the Cumberland Pacquet, Whitehaven, 6 copies.
White, Sampson, Esq. Gough Square.
Whitmarsh, George, surgeon, Wilton.
Workman, M. surgeon, Basingstoke.
Walford, Thomas, Esq. Whitley Birdbrook.
Williams, Rev. J. Basingstoke.
Woolston, T. Adderbury.
Wilkinson, Thomas, Esq. Barbican.
Wilkes, John, Esq. Milland-house, Sussex.
Wilkes, John, junior, Esq. Inner Temple.
Watts, Joseph, printer, Gosport.
Windover, Nicholas, Basingstoke.
Were, Robert, Garratt, Surry.
Were, William, Wandsworth.
Were, Samuel, Union Street, Southwark.
Wilson, Andrew, printer, London.

Young, Thomas, M.D. F.R.S.

PANTOGRAPHIA.

Abyssinian.

Abbahn schirfifu. Selenskgi zebonsha. Meff-haq spirsa. Ischir jergash. Semskan hirman egahquahn. Parchon pmlegron; ha parchons phlegonaos. Ne hibli kan scepi kha. Erupn ihapsa. Abbahn schirfifu. Selenskgi zebon-sha, Meffahq spirsa. Ischir jergash. Semskan hirman egahquahn. Parchon pmlegron.

Amharic.

Abâtâtyn bassamaj jalach. Jynzalyn mangys-tcha. Fakâdychm jyhuyn bassamaj yndalach-schig bamydram. Sisâjâtyn yjaylatu zâre sy-tan. Badalâtyn myharan ynjam jabadalanan yndo nymhyr. Hamansut nygabâ matan at-tawan. Adhanan yndu kabis nagar. Ysma ziaka jyy'ti mengy'st hajl wasybhat laalama a

Angolan.

Tota a monte. 1. Hosa azure. 2. Macla agisa. 3. Anfonsa ara quereola azureta o amano. 4. Afonnimonte iouro toma mon-tiouro a fauco. 5. O augamont plecha mon almont augumos plechomont. 6. Ouan-mont-cault plutech. 7. Si auermont moiue. Amin.

Abyssinian.

This is the language of one of the provinces of Ethiopia, of which there are many, all varying much in their dialect, but using the same character.---See Ethiopic.

The ſpecimen given is a version of the Lord's Prayer.

Orat. Dom. p. 26.

Amharic.

This is also one of the provincial tongues of Ethiopia, which are particularly noticed in Bruce's Travels, vol. 1, p. 401.—It is a version of the Lord's Prayer.

Orat. Dom. p. 15.

Angolan.

The Lord's Prayer.

Orat. Dom. p. 25.

ARABIC 1.

ܐ ܒ ܓ ܕ ܗ ܘ ܙ ܚ ܛ ܝ ܟ ܠ

l c i t ch z v h d g b a

ܡ ܢ ܣ ܥ ܦ ܨ ܩ ܪ ܫ ܛ̈ ܬ̈ ܟ̇

ch th tz sc r k ts ph hh s n m

ܕ̇ ܨ̇ ܛ̇ ܥ̇ ܠܐ

la gc thz dz dh

ARABIC 2.

ا ـا ب بـ ـبـ ـب ت تـ ـتـ ـت ث ثـ ـثـ ـث

T T B A

ج جـ ـجـ ـج ح حـ ـحـ ـح خ خـ ـخـ ـخ د ـد ذ ـذ

D D Ch Hh G

ر ـر ز ـز س سـ ـسـ ـس ش شـ ـشـ ـش ص صـ ـصـ ـص

S Sj S Z R

ض ضـ ـضـ ـض ط ـط ظ ـظ ع عـ ـعـ ـع غ غـ ـغـ ـغ

G Ai D T D

ف فـ ـفـ ـف ق قـ ـقـ ـق ك كـ ـكـ ـك ل لـ ـلـ ـل

L C K F

م مـ ـمـ ـم ن نـ ـنـ ـن و ـو ه هـ ـهـ ـه ي يـ ـيـ ـي

I H W N M

ARABIC 1.

The most ancient Arabic Letters are the Kufic, so named from the City of Kufa on the Euphrates; (Encyc. Franc. des Alph. anc. et mod. Pl. 3.) but they do not appear to be in use at this time.—This alphabet was communicated to Dr. Morton of the British Museum, by Dr. Hunt, Hebrew and Arabic Professor at Oxford, from the Bodleian Library.

Dr. Morton's Tables.

ARABIC 2.

These modern Characters are the invention of the Vizier Molach, who flourished about 933 of the Christian Æra, with which he wrote the Koran three times, and in a manner so fair and correct, as to be considered a perfect model of writing it.

Fourn. v. 2. p. 278.

This is the common character of the TURKS and PERSIANS, but these people have five more letters than the ARABS, (Fourn. v. 2. p. 278,) which I shall give in their proper places. This is the alphabet in present use, in which are expressed the Initials, Medials, and Finals; with their powers subjoined.

Arabic 3.

أَبُونَا ٱلَّذِي فِي ٱلسَّمٰوَاتِ،

1. لِيَتَقَدَّسِ ٱسْمُكَ،

2. لِتَأْتِ مَلَكُوتُكَ،

3. لِتَكُنْ مَشِيئَتُكَ كَمَا فِي ٱلسَّمَاءِ وَعَلَي ٱلْأَرْضِ،

4. خُبْزَنَا كَفَافَنَا أَعْطِنَا فِي ٱلْيَوْمِ

5. وَٱغْفِرْ لَنَا خَطَايَانَا كَمَا نَغْفِرُ نَحْنُ لِمَنْ أَخْطَأَ إِلَيْنَا،

6. وَلَا تُدْخِلْنَا ٱلتَّجَارِبَ.

7. لَكِنْ نَجِّنَا مِنَ ٱلشِّرِّيرِ،

* لِأَنَّ لَكَ ٱلْمُلْكَ وَٱلْقُوَّةَ وَٱلْمَجْدَ إِلَي ٱلْأَبَدِ،

أَمِينَ

Arabic 4.

ch	z	v	h	d	g	b	a
hh	s	n	m	l	c	i	t
thz	dz	dh	sc	r	k	ts	ph

Arabic 3.

Is the Lord's Prayer in the same character, of which the literal reading is to be seen in No. 6.

Orat. Dom. p. 16.

Arabic 4.

Or *Mauritanian*. This alphabet is used in Morocco and Fez, and the northern parts of Africa.

Fourn. v. 2. p. 279.

Arabic 5.

l c i t ch z v h d g b a

gc tz dz sc r k ts ph hh s n m

dh ch th tz

Arabic 6.

Ya Abanalladi phissamawati. Yatakaddasu smoca. Tati malacutoca. Tacuno mashiatoca Cama phissamai wa ala'l ardi. Chubzana'lladi lil gadi ahtinaol yaum. Waghphir lana ma aleina. Cama naghphiro nahno liman lana alcihi. Wala tudkilna hagiarib. Lakin naggina minnash shirriti. Lianna leka'lmulka, va'lkou

Armenian 1.

ա բ գ դ ե զ է ը թ ժ ի լ

a b g d ie z e é th j i l

խ ծ կ հ ձ ղ ճ մ յ ն շ պ

ch dz k h ds gh tc m ï n sch p

ո չ ջ ռ ս վ տ ր ց ւ փ ֆ

o tch dch rr s w t r ts y ph f

ARABIC 5.

Known by the general name of African.

Fourn. v. 2. p. 279.

ARABIC 6.

The literal reading of the Lord's Prayer, which is in the original character in No. 3.

Wilk. Ess. p. 435.

ARMENIAN 1.

The Armenian language approaches near to the Chaldean and Syriac; many parts of it are common with other orientals, the Greek, and that of the Gauls, which renders the pronunciation difficult. It is used, not only in Great and Little Armenia, but in Asia Minor, Syria, Tartary, Persia, and other nations. Duret, p. 725.

This is the character used for the fine printing of this language.

Dr. Morton's Tables.

Armenian 2.

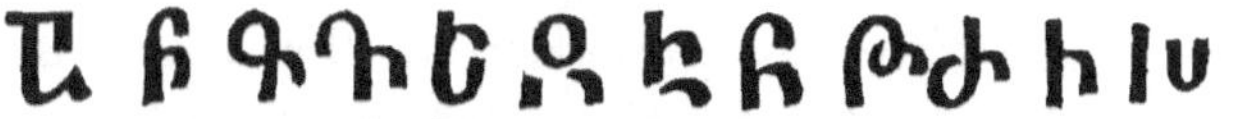

a b g d ie z e é th j i ch

dz k h ds gh tc m ï n sch o tch

p dch rr s w t r ts y ph kh f

Armenian 3.

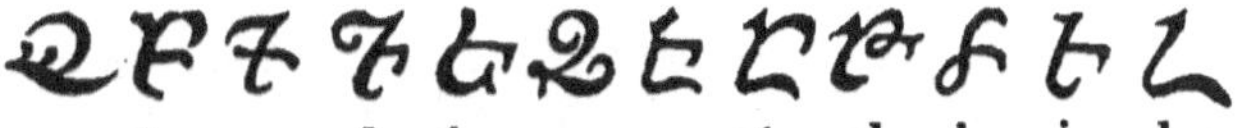

a b g d ie z e é th j i l

ch dz k h ds gh tc m ï n sch o

tch p dch rr s w t r ts y ph kh

Armenian 4.

a b g d ie z e é th j i l

ch dz k h ds gh tc m ï n sch o

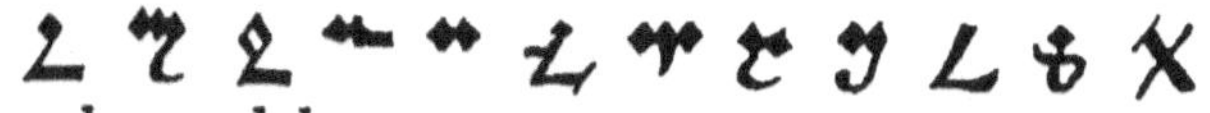

tch p dch rr s w t r ts y ph kh

Armenian 2.

This letter was used to ornament the frontispieces and titles of books; also for public inscriptions, whence the French have given it the name of *Lapidaire*.

Fourn. v. 2. p. 276.

Armenian 3.

These are the capital letters of their common writing, taken from their books. Some authors suppose that this character was invented by St. Chrysostom, who was banished by the Emperor, from Constantinople into Armenia, where he died.

Fourn. v. 2. p. 276.

Armenian 4.

The lower-case alphabet, or small letters to the preceding.

Fourn. v. 2. p. 276.

ARMENIAN 5.

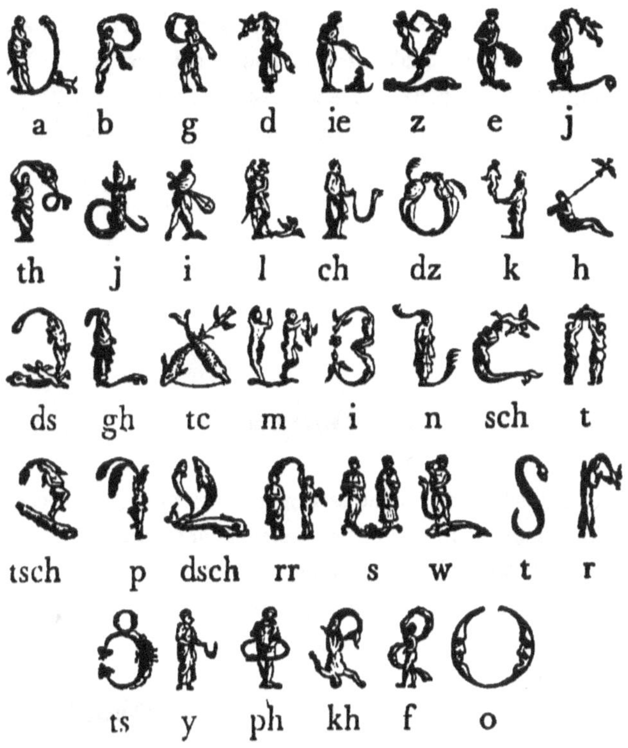

ARMENIAN 6.

a b g d ie z ĕ j th z i l

ē ds q h x gl gh m ï n sh o

z p sc rh s w t r tz y ps ch

ARMENIAN 5.

These letters are termed blooming or flowery, and are used in titles of books, and as two-line letters in the beginnings of chapters. They represent flowers, and the figures of men and animals, and in shape are formed like the *Lapidaire*, No. 2.

Encyc. Fr. pl. 12 and 13.

ARMENIAN 6.

In Schröder's Thesaurus Linguæ Armenicæ, the French Encyclopedie in folio, and other books, we meet with the five preceding Armenian alphabets only, but Duret gives this as the first used by this people, taken from the letters of an inscription over a large entrance into the castle of Curcho.

Duret, p. *725.*

Armenian 7.

Hair mer or iercins des. Surb eglizzi a nun cho. Eceszzæ archaiuthai cho. Eglizzin cam cho. Orpes jercins en jercri. Zhazt mer hanapazord rue mez aisaur. Eu thogl mez zpaartis mer. Orpas eu mech thoglumch merozt partpanazt. Eu mi tanir zmezi phorxuthai. Ail pharceai zmez izaræ. Amin.

Aremorican 1.

Hon tat pehing son in acou'n. Oth hano bezet sanctifiet. De vel de ompho rouantelez. Ha volonté bezet gret voar an douar evel en coûn. Roit dezomp hinou hor bara bemdezier, ha pardon nil dezomp hon offançon evel ma pardon nomp d'ac re odeus hon offançet. Ha n'hon digaçit quel è tentation. Hogen de livrit a drove. Amen.

Aremorican 2.

Hon tad pehudij sou en efaou, da hanou bezet sanctifiet. Devet aornomp da rouantelaez Da eol bezet graet en douar, eual maz eon en euf. Ró dimp hyziou hon bara pemdeziec. Pardon dimp hon pechedou, eual ma pardonomp da nep pegant ezomp offanzet. Há na dilaes quet a hanomp en temptation. Hoguen

ARMENIAN 7.

The Lord's Prayer.

Wilk. Ess. p. 435.

AREMORICAN 1. AND 2.

Two versions of the Lord's prayer, formerly used in that part of France called Aremorica; (Orat. Dom. p. 51,) lately Brittany, or Bretagne; but now forming the five departments of the *North-coast*, *Finisterre*, *Ille and Villaine*, *Lower Loire*, and *Morbiham*.

ATOOI.

Tehaia	*Where*	He oho	*The hair*
E poo	*The head*	Matta	*The eye*
Haieea	*Fish*	Waheine	*A woman*
Haire	*To go*	Tooanna	*A brother*
Erooi	*To puke*	Too	*Sugar cane*
My, ty	*Good*	Matou	*I*
Oohe	*Yams*	Booa	*A hog*
Tanata	*A man*	Pahoo	*A drum*
Eeneeoo	*Cocoa nuts*	Ehoora	*A dance*
Eroemy	*Fetch it*	Ooroo	*Bread fruit*
Matte	*Dead*	Aoonai	*Presently*
Paha	*Perhaps*	Ai	*Yes*
Noona	*Above*	Poore	*A prayer*
Tahouna	*A priest*	Aiva	*A harbour*
Motoo	*An island*	Hai, raa	*The sun*
Hairanee	*The sky*	Harre	*A house*
Eatooa	*A god*	Homy	*Give me*

BALI.

ca khá kha ga ta da ta

na thá da ba ua ka kaa ki

1 2 3 4 5 6 7 8 9

Atooi.

Is one of the Sandwich Islands in the South Seas, discovered by Captain Cook; they consist of a group, extending in lat. from 18° 54′ to 22° 15′ north; and in long. from 199 36′ to 205° 6′ east. This specimen of the language is taken from the vocabulary.

Cook's laſt Voy. vol. 3. p. 549.

Bali.

Is an island north of Java, populous and abounding with rice and fruits.—Lat. 7° 10′ ſouth; long. 215° 50′ eaſt.

This character is taken from the Encyc. Franc. des Alph. anc. et mod. pl. 21.

BASTARD.

Aa Bb Cc Dd Ee Ff Gg Hh

a b c d e f g h

Ii Kk Ll Mm Nn Oo Pp Qq

i k l m n o p q

Rr ꝛ Sſs Tt Uu v X y y Zz &

r s t u v x y z &

BENGALLEE.

thŏ tŏ iun zhŏ zŏ shŏ sŏ uang

ghŏ gŏ khŏ kŏ bhŏ bŏ phŏ nŏ

dhŏ dŏ thŏ tŏ anŏ dhŏ dŏ khiŏ

BERRYAN.

Nouestre pere que sias dins l'ou Ciel, vouestre nom siet santifia. Que vouestre royame nous arribe. Que vouestre volonta siet fache, a la comme a ou Ciel. Dona nous aujourdhuy nuestre pan quotidien. Et perdona nos nuestros offenses, como nos outros pardonem a na quoties que nous en offensa. Et ne nous lais-

Bastard.

This letter was in common use in France in the 14th and 15th centuries, and called Bastard, or Mongrel, being derived from the *Lettres de forme*, which it resembles, but has most of its angles cut off, or much lessened. It was first made by a German, named Heilmann, in 1490.

Fourn. v. 2. p. 265.

Bengallee.

This is the character used in the extensive country of Bengal, now subject to the English East-India Company. It was copied from pl. 18 of the Encyc. Franc. des Alph. anc. et mod.

Berryan.

Berry was a province of France, but now forms the two departments of *Cher* and *Indre;* it is very fertile in corn, wine, fruits, hemp, and flax.

The specimen given is the Lord's Prayer, (Orat. Dom. p. 39,) which seems to be only a dialect of the French.

Biscayan.

Gure aita cerue tan aicena. Sanctifica bedi hire ieena. Et hoz bedi hire rehuma. Eguin bedi hire vozondatea cervan be cala lurrean ere. Gure egoneco oguia igue egun. Eta quit ta jetrague gure cozrac: Nola gucre gure cozduney quittatzen baitra vegu. Eta ezgai zalasar eracitenta tentacione tan. Baima delibza gaitzac gaich totic.

Bohemian.

Otozie nass genz syna nebesich. Oszwiet se meno twe. Przid kralowstwii twe. Bud wule twa. Yakona nebi tak y na zeni. Chleb nasz wezdeyssi dey nam dnes. Yodpust nam nasse winy. Yako y my odpaustime nassim winikom. Y ne uwod nasz do pokussenii. Ale zbaw nas od zleho.

Ancient British 1.

Eyen taad rhuvn wytyn y neofoedodd; Santeiddier yr hemuv tau: De vedy dyrnas dau: Guueler dy wollys arryddayar megis agyn y nefi. Eyn bara beunydda vul dyro inniheddivu: Ammaddeu ynny evn deledion, megis agi maddevu in deledvvir ninaw: Agna thowys ni in brofedigaeth: Namyn gvvaredni

Biscayan.

Biscay is a province of Spain, but the language seems not to have any affinity to that of the nation. The Biscayers are of Celtic extraction, and still preserve their peculiar language, the *Basque*, which is different from any other in Europe.

Walker's Gazetteer.

The specimen given is the Lord's Prayer.

Wilk. Ess. p. 435.

Bohemian.

The Lord's Prayer.

Wilk. Ess. p. 435.

Ancient British 1.

The Lord's Prayer.

Orat. Dom. p. 50.

Ancient British 2.

Ein tad yr hwn wytl yn y nesoedd. Sanctedidier dy enw. Deued dy deyrnas. Bid dy ewyllys ar yddaiar, megis y mae yn y nefoed. Dyro i ni heddyw ein bara beunyddiol, amad deu i ni ein dyledion, fel a maddeuwn ni in dyledwgr. Ac nac arwain ni i brofe digaeth. Eithr gwared ni rhag drwg. Amen.

Bulgarian.

a b v g d e x z

dz i k l m n o p

r s t y f ps sch ia

Bullantic.

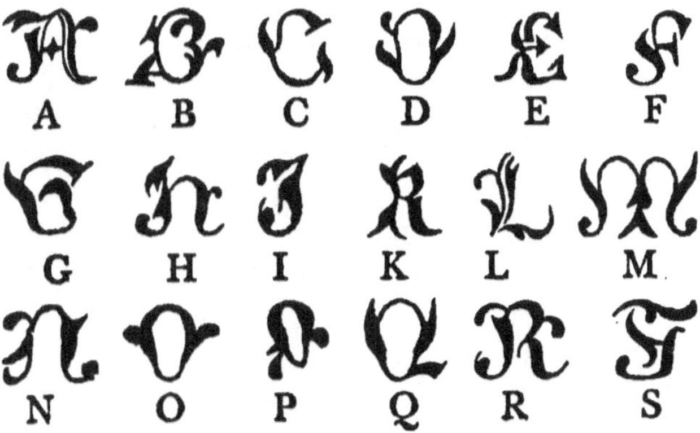

Ancient British 2.

The Lord's Prayer, given as more modern than the former.

Wilk. Ess. p. 435.

Bulgarian.

Bulgaria is a province of Turkey; the character favors much of the Illyrian, (Fourn. v. 2. p. 275,) but the dialect is Sclavonian.

Bullantic.

Capital ornamented letters in use for the dispatch of the Apoſtolic Bulls.

Fourn. v. 2. p. 269.

CADEAUX.

CARNISH.

Ozha nash kir si v'nebesih. Posvezhenu bodi iime tvoie. Pridi k'nam kraylestvu tvoie. S'i-dise volia tvoia. Kakor nanebi taku nasemlij. Kruh nash usak dainii dai nam dones. Inu odpusti nam dulge nashe. Kakor tudi mi odpustimo dulshnikom nashim. Inu neupelai nas v'iskushno. Tamazh reshi nass od slega. Sakai tvoje je krailestvu, múzh, zhhast veko-

CATALONIAN.

Pare nostro, que estau en lo cel. Sanctificat sea el vostre sant nom. Vinga en nos altres el vostra saint reine. Fasas la vostra voluntat, axi en la terra como se fa en lo cel. El pa nostre de cada dia da nous lo gui. I perdonau nos nostres culpes; axi como nos altres perdonam a nostres deudores. I no permetau

Cadeaux.

Capital flourishing letters used in ancient French writings of the 5th century.

Fourn. v. 2. p. 269.

Carnish.

Or, of the *Carni*, inhabitants of Carniola, a province of Germany.

This is the Lord's Prayer.

Wilk. Ess. p. 435.

Catalonian.

The Lord's Prayer.

Orat. Dom. p. 36.

Celtic.

'S e guth anaim mo ruin a tha 'nn,
O! 's ainmach gu aislin Mhalmhin' thu,
Fosgluibh-se talla nan speur,
Aithra Oscair nan cruaidh-bheum;
Fosgluibh-se doirsa nan nial,
Tha ceumma Mhalmhine go dian.
Chualam guth a' m' aislin fein,
Tha fathrum mo chleibh go ard.
C' uime thanic an Ossag a' m' dheigh
O dhubh-shiubhal na linne od thall?
Bha do sgiath shuimnach ann gallan aon-
Shiubhall aislin Mhalmhine go dian, [aich,
Ach chunic is' a run ag aomadh,
'S a cheo-earradh ag aomadh m' a chliabh:
Bha dearsa na greine air thaobh ris,
Co boisgal ri or nan daimh.
'S e guth anaim mo ruin a tha 'nn,
O! 's ainmach gu m' aislin fein thu.
'S comhnuidh dhuit anam Mhalmhine,
Mhic Ossain is treine lamh.

Ceram.

Oeenta	Olooa	Otoloo	Opatoo	Oleema
1	2	3	4	5
Oloma	Opeeto	Oaloo	Oteeo	Opooloo
6	7	8	9	10

CELTIC.

This language, under all it's disadvantages from the subjecting powers of Greece and Rome; and afterwards from Saxon innovations in this country, is still spoken with much purity upon a great part of the continent, and in the islands of Scotland; and it exists at this day one of the greatest living monuments of antiquity.

The annexed specimen of it is taken from *Malvina's Dream*, by OSSIAN, of which the following is a translation in English.

Shaw's Anal. p. 157.

TRANSLATION:

" It was the voice of my love! few are his visits to the " Dreams of Malvina! Open your airy halls, ye fathers of " mighty Toscar! unfold the gates of your clouds.—The steps " of Malvina's departure are nigh.—I have heard a voice in " my dream.—I feel the fluttering of my soul.—Why didst thou " come, O blast, from the dark rolling of the lake? Thy rust" ling was in the trees, the dream of Malvina departed.—But " she beheld her love, when his robe of mist flew on the wind; " the beam of the sun was on his skirts, they glittered like the " gold of the stranger.—It was the voice of my love; few are " his visits to Malvina.

" But thou dwellest in the soul of Malvina, son of mighty " Ossian."

CERAM

Is one of the Molucca isles.—Sydney Parkinson gives the annexed vocabulary of numeration, but is silent as to their general language.

P. 200.

CHALDEAN 1.

hh z v h d g b a

o s n m l k i th

t sch r q ts p

CHALDEAN 2.

hh z v h d g b a

o s n m l k i th

t sch r q ts p

CHALDEAN 3.

hh z v h d g b a

o s n m l k i th

t sch r q ts p

Chaldean.

Chaldea, or Babylonia, a kingdom of Asia, and the most ancient in the world, was founded by Nimrod, the son of Cush, and grandson of Ham, who, according to some historians, built Nineveh, the capital of Assyria.

Philologists are much divided in their sentiments or opinions, respecting the antiquity of this language.

Pliny informs us, that Gellius attributed letters to the Egyptian Mercury, and others, to the Syrians.

The learned Roman just mentioned, supposed that the Assyrian letters were prior to any record of history, and by these he undoubtedly meant the Chaldean: it should seem most probable, that the language used by the antediluvian Patriarchs, bore the greatest analogy to this, especially when it is universally allowed that they inhabited that part of the globe, whence many have thought the Chaldean to have been prior to the Samaritan and Hebrew.

See Preface.

Chaldean 1.

Called *Cælestial;* said to have been composed by the ancient astrologers, from the figures of certain stars; and represented in two hemispheres. Gaffarel, p. 1.

Chaldean 2.

Theseus Ambrosius asserts, that this character was brought from Heaven by the Angel Raphael, by whom it was communicated to Adam, who used it in composing Psalms after his expulsion from the terrestrial paradise.

Some authors pretend that Moses and the prophets used this letter, and that they were forbidden to divulge it to mortal men. Duret, p. 119.

Chaldean 3.

This character is also said to have been used by Adam.

Spanh. Dissert. p. 80.
Dr. Morton's Tables.

Chaldean 4.

Chaldean 5.

hh z v h d g b a

o s n m l k i th

t sch r q ts p

Chaldean 6.

hh z v h d g b a

aa s n m l k i th

t sch r q ts p

Chaldean 4.

Brought from the Holy Land to Venice, when the christian princes made war against the infidels; this is a handsome letter, and it is said, was the same that Seth engraved upon the two columns, mentioned in chap. 4 of the first book of Josephus. It it also said, that there is, in Ethiopia, a treatise on divine subjects, written in this character by Enoch, which is preserved with great care, and considered as canonical.

This is given as a Hebrew, but without any explanation of the power of each letter.

Duret, p. 127.

Chaldean 5.

This character is said to have been used by Noah.

Spanh. Dissert. p. 80.

Chaldean 6.

Attributed to Ninus, the first King of the Assyrians.

Spanh. Dissert. p. 80.

Chaldean 7.

Chaldean 8.

Chaldean 9.

hh z v h d g b a

o s n m l k i th

t sch r q ts p ph

Chaldean 7.

This is said to have been used by Abraham.

Spanh. Dissert. p. 80.

Chaldean 8.

Copied from ancient marbles brought from the Holy Land, and are asserted to have been used by Abraham.

Duret, p. 126.

Chaldean 9.

This character is represented as the same on which the tables of the law that were given to Moses, were written, and are known to the Hebrews under the name of *Malachim*, or *Mĕlachim*.

Duret, p. 123.

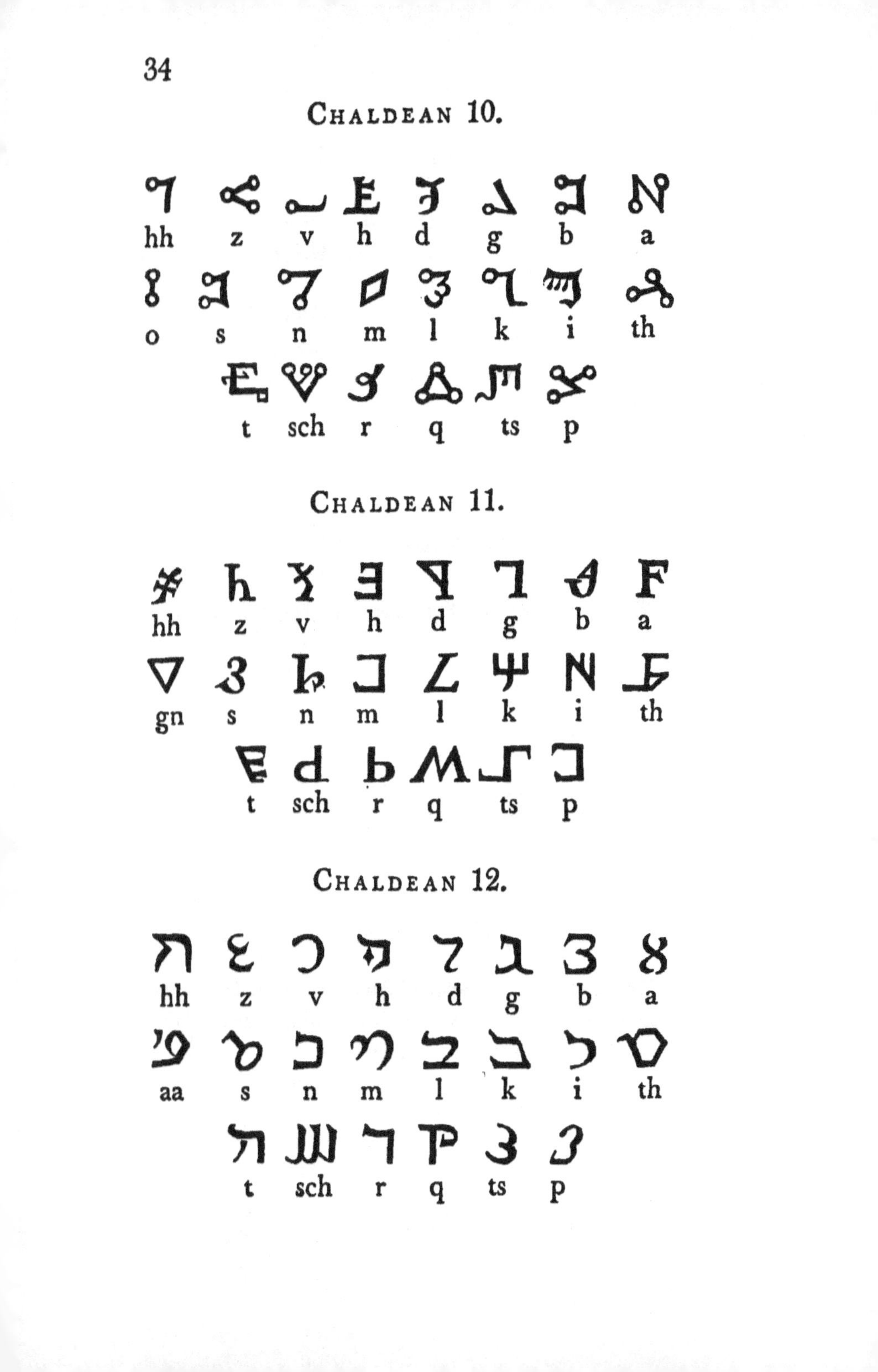

Chaldean 10.

hh z v h d g b a

o s n m l k i th

t sch r q ts p

Chaldean 11.

hh z v h d g b a

gn s n m l k i th

t sch r q ts p

Chaldean 12.

hh z v h d g b a

aa s n m l k i th

t sch r q ts p

Chaldean 10.

Sigismond Fante says, that this alphabet is of very great antiquity, having been used by the Hebrews in the wilderness, in the time of Moses.

De Sivry's Recherches, p. 191.

Duret, p. 124, says, this character was given to Abraham, when he departed from Chaldea for the Land of Canaan.

Chaldean 11.

Fournier calls this a Phenician alphabet, but attributes it to Moses.

Vol. 2, p. 280.

Chaldean 12.

Or ancient Hebrew, which is also supposed to have been used in the time of Moses, and from which, most of the other Chaldean alphabets are derived.

Fourn. v. 2. p. 280.

Chaldean 13.

t sch r q ts p o

Chaldean 14.

hh z v h d g b a

s n m l k i th

t sch r q ts p o

Chaldean 15.

hh z v h d g b a

s n m l l k i th

t sch r q ts p o

Chaldean 13.

This character is used by a nation of Mesopotamia, called *Bagadet*, now under the Turkish dominion.

Duret, p. 345.
Fourn. v. 2. p. 279.

Chaldean 14.

Theseus Ambrosius, in his treatise on various languages and characters, calls this *Judaic*.

Duret, p. 335.

Fournier, v. 2. p. 279, ſays, that it was used by the Jews during their captivity in Babylon.

Chaldean 15.

This character was much used in Persia and Media, and by the Jewish inhabitants of Babylon.

Duret, p. 344.
Fourn. v. 2. p. 278.

Chaldean 16.

a b g d e z h th

i k l m n x ŏ p

r s t u ph ch ps ō

Chaldean 17.

v z v z d g v e

f p n l h c h t

t r s r k a s p

Chaldean 18.

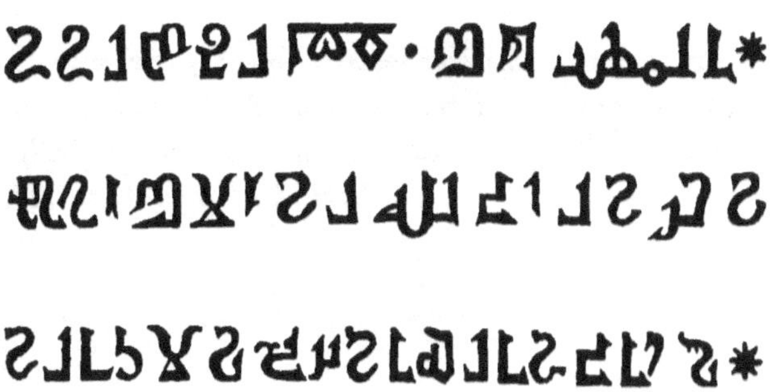

CHALDEAN 16.

This alphabet was found in the Grimani library at Venice, and contrary to all other Chaldeans, is written from left to right.

Some authors assert that this is the character of the Maronites, inhabitants of Asia, on the borders of the Red Sea.

Duret, p. 346.

CHALDEAN 17.

Jean Baptiste Palatin, a Roman citizen, in one of his books in Italian, upon the manner of writing all sorts of letters, both ancient and modern, gives this as an ancient Chaldean.

Duret, p. 347.

CHALDEAN 18.

The copy of a Chaldean inscription, very curiously cut in the square stones of the tower of Baych, over one of the gates of the very ancient city of Panormus, in Sicily.

Fazelli Rer. Sicular, p. 149.

Chaldean 19.

אבונא דבשמיא: יתקדש שמך: תאתא מלכותך
יהוא צבינך כמא בשמיא כנמא בארעא:
הב־־לז להמא דמסתנא ביומא: ושבק לז הובי
כמא אנז שבקנא להיבי: ואל תעלז לנסיונא:
אלא פצא יתז מז בישא: מטול רדילך איתיה
מלכותא והילא ותשבוהא לעלמיז: אבונא דבשם
יתקדש שמך: תאתא מלכותך: יהוא צבינך כמא

Chaldean 20.

Abhouna debhischmaija; jithkaddasch schemach; tethe malchouthach; jehĕveh tsibhjanach kma bhischmaija knema bh-ar-a; habhlan lahhma dmissetana bhjoma; uschebuk lan hhobai kma anan schbhakna bĕhhai jabhai; v'al thaălan lenissajona; ella phza jathan min bischa; m'toul dĕdhilach iteeh malchutha vehhéla vetheschbuhha l'a'lmin. Amen.

Charlemagne 1.

a b c d e f g h

i k l m n o p q

r s t u x y z &

CHALDEAN 19.

The Lord's Prayer.

Orat. Dom. p. 11.

CHALDEAN 20.

The literal version of the above.

Orat. Dom. p. 11.

CHARLEMAGNE 1.

This great Emperor, who restored learning to Italy, France, and Germany, encouraged the formation of good letters in his dominions; those in use having degenerated into bad imitations of the shape of the Lombard, Saxon, and Franco-Gallic.

These three alphabets are attributed to this monarch, and bear his name; they appeared early in the ninth century.

Fourn. v. 2. p. 272.

We observe that he did not think the distinction of capitals and small letters necessary in his alphabets.

Charlemagne 2.

Charlemagne 3.

Chinese 1.

Ngo tem fu che tsay thiæn. Ngo tem yuen ul niun chim xim. Ul gue lin. Ul chi chim him. Yu ty su sim thyæn. Ngo teng uwang uul kyn jun ngo ngo zie jong leang. Uul my æn ong-o tsi ay. Ziu ngo ije ssa tou ngo tsi ay tsie. Yeeu pu ngo chiu chi eu iu ieau can Nay kyeea ngo yu chiu'o.

Charlemagne 2 and 3.

See the last article.

Chinese 1.

Version of the Lord's Prayer.

Wilk. Ess. p. 485.

Chinese 2.

黹	馬	隶	赤	色	网
tchì	mà	tái	tchĕ	sĕ	vàng
黽	骨	隹	走	艸	羊
min	kŏ	tchōui	tçèou	tçào	yang
鼎	高	雨	足	虍	羽
ting	cāo	yù	tçŏ	hoù	yoù
鼓	髟	青	身	虫	老
kòu	piēou	tsing	chīn	tchông	laò

Coptic 1.

Ⲁ	Ⲃ	Ⲅ	Ⲇ	Ⲉ	Ⲍ	Ⲋ	Ⲏ
a	b	g	d	e	z	s	h
Ⲑ	Ⲓ	Ⲕ	Ⲗ	Ⲙ	Ⲛ	Ⲝ	Ⲟ
th	i	k	l	m	n	x	o
Ⲡ	Ⲣ	Ⲥ	Ⲧ	Ⲩ	Ⲫ	Ⲭ	Ⲯ
p	r	s	t	y	ph	ch	ps

Chinese 2.

This language has no alphabet, being composed of a great number of very limited sounds, and it would be impossible to understand it in any other character. It has but 328 sounds, and all monosyllables, applicable to 80,000 characters, of which this language is composed.

There are also 214 keys, or radical characters, the whole of which are given, correctly and beautifully engraved, in the Encyc. Franc. pl. 25, whence the annexed specimen is copied.

Coptic 1.

This character, which Fournier calls an *ancient* Coptic, was used by the inhabitants of a city of Egypt, called Coptos; whence the Cophtites derived their origin. They were christians, and flourished in great numbers in the time of Dioclesian, who put many to death, and sent the rest into exile.

V. 2. p. 274.
Duret, p. 755.

Coptic 2.

Ⲁⲁ	Ⲃⲃ	Ⲅⲅ	Ⲇⲇ	Ⲉⲉ	Ⲋⲋ	Ⲍⲍ	Ⲏⲏ
a	b	g	d	ĕ	s	z	ē
Ⲑⲑ	Ⲓⲓ	Ⲕⲕ	Ⲗⲗ	Ⲙⲙ	Ⲛⲛ	Ⲝⲝ	Ⲟⲟ
th	i	k	l	m	n	x	o
Ⲡⲡ	Ⲣⲣ	Ⲥⲥ	Ⲧⲧ	Ⲩⲩ	Ⲫⲫ	Ⲭⲭ	Ⲯⲯ
p	r	s	t	u	ph	ch	ps

Coptic 3.

Theut habh atast en ornos. Plenspliah arich eho. Abspinth bahl eho. Erup vlid heo ah en orna, si ben isi. Beko bibh pueum, thet hio memah. Fib aff hla ihos gipsa hio; omsh afflom gipsam hia. Sib auk quarb en zharafhi, as afsh hio malach. Amin.

Coptic 4.

Peniot etchennipheoui. Mareftoubonje pecran. Maresinje tecme touro. Netehnacmarefshopi. Phredichentphenemhi jenpicahi. Fenoiki terasti meifnanphoou. Ouohchanieteron nanebolmphretitio. Tenchoebol neete. Ouo omper tenechou epirasmos. Alla nah menebolch enpipethmou.

Coptic 2.

This character has a very great affinity to the Greek, from which it evidently appears to have been formed, and was introduced into Egypt, under the successors of Alexander. The Coptic language, which is only to be met with in the books of the christians of Egypt, is a mixture of the Greek, and the ancient Egyptian tongue, and was used by them in their translations of the sacred writings, church books, &c.

Enc. Franc. pl. 7.
Fourn. v. 2. p. 274.

Coptic 3.

The Lord's Prayer.

Orat. Dom. p. 25.

Coptic 4.

The Lord's Prayer.

Wilk. Ess. p. 435.

Cornish.

Ny taz ez yn neau. Bonegas yw tha hanaw. Tha Gwlakath doaz. Tha bonogath bogweez eņ nore pocoragen neau. Roe thenyen dythma gon dyth bara givians. Ny gan rabn weery cara ny givians mens. O cabin ledia ny nara idn tentation. Buz dilver ny thart doeg. Amen.

Croatian.

Ozhe nash ishe efina nebesih. Svetise jme tuoę. Pridi cesa rastvo tvuoe. Budi volia tvoja Jako na niebesih j tako nasemlij. Hlib nash usag danni dai nam danas. Jodpusti nam dlgi nashe. Jaco she imi odpushzhamo dishnikom nashim. Ine isbavi nas od nepriasni. Dais bavi nas od sla.

Dalmatian 1.

a b v g d e x z

tz i i y k l m n

o p r s t u ph ch

CORNISH.

The Lord's Prayer.

Orat. Dom. p. 52.

CROATIAN.

The Lord's Prayer.

Wilk. Ess. p. 435.

The character used by the Croats is the same as the ILLYRIAN 1, which see.

The languages of this people, the DALMATIANS, ILLYRIANS, SCLAVONS, &c., situated in this part of Europe, are pronounced much like that of Italy.

DALMATIAN 1.

This character is said to have been invented by St. Jerom. It is very difficult to pronounce, yet many missals, and the breviary from the Latin; and even the Old and New Testaments, have been translated into it from the Hebrew and Greek.

Duret, p. 738.

Dalmatian 2.

Otsce nas koyi-yessina nebissih. Szvetisse gyme tvoye. Pridi kralyess tvo tvoze. Budi volya tvoya: kako na nebu, tako ina zemlyi. Kruh nas ssvagdanyni day nam danass. Jod pussti naam duge nase. Kako i my odpuschyamo duxnikom nassim. Ine naass uvediu-napasst. Da osslobodi naas od assla. Amen.

Danish.

Pader vor du som est i himmelen. Helligt vorde dit naffn. Til komme dit rige. Borde din billie; saa paa jorden som hand er i himmelen. Giff oz i dag vort daglige brod. Oc forlad oz skyld; som wi forlade vore skyldener. Oc leed oz icke voi fristelse. Men frels oz fra ont. Thi rigit er dit, oc krafft, oc herligved ewighed. Amen.

Domesday.

Rex ten̄ in dn̄ic W letone. T. R. E. 7 m̄ se defd̄ p. xi hid̄. Tra. ē. xi. car. In dn̄io e una car. 7 xv. uilli 7 xmi. bord̄ cu. x̄. car. Ibi. iii. serui. 7 ii. molini pe. vw. solid. 7 viii. ac q̄ti· silva qte ē in chent. Richard de Tonebrige ten̄ de hoc m una uirgatacn silva. und̄e abstulit custicum qui ibi mrnehat. No

Dalmatian 2.

The Lord's Prayer.

Wilk. Ess. p. 435.

Danish.

The Lord's Prayer.

Wilk. Ess. p. 435.
Orat. Dom. p. 55.

Domesday.

This character was cut by the late ingenious Thomas Cotterel, the letter founder, for the folio edition of Domesday book.

The specimen given is taken from Luckombe's history of the origin and progress of printing; 8vo. Lond. 1770. p. 174.

High Dutch.

Unser Vater, der du bist im himmel, geheiliget werd dein name. Zukomme dein reich. Dein wille geschehe, wie im himmel also auch auf erden. Unser tâglich brodt gib uns heute. Und vergib uns unser schuld, als wir vergeben unsern schuldigern. Unde fuhre uns nict in versuchung. Sondern erlô se uns von dem bosen. Den dein is das reich, und die krafft,

Low Dutch 1.

Onse vader die in den hemelin; uwen naem werde geheylight; uw coninckrijcke icome; uwen wille geschiede, gelijck in den hemel oockop der aerden; ons daghelijcks broot gheeft ons heden; ende vergheeft ons onse scoulden, gelijck vock wy vergheven onsen, schuldenaren; ende en leydtons nict in ver-

Low Dutch 2.

Onse Vader, die in de hemelin zyn uwen naam worde gèheylight; uw'koningryk kome; uwe wille geschiede gelyck in den hemel zoo ook op den arden, ons dagelicks broot geef ons heeden endevergeeft onse schulden gelyk ook wy vergeeven onso schuldenaaren: ende en laat ons neet in versoer kingemaer vertost on van der hoosen. Amen.

High Dutch.

Or the German, is a dialect of the Teutonic.

The specimen given is the Lord's Prayer in the modern tongue.

Guthrie, p. 746.

Low Dutch 1.

The Lord's Prayer.

Wilk. Ess. p. 435.

This language is spoken in the Seven United Provinces, and is compounded of the Teutonic, French, and Latin.

Guthrie, p. 728.

Low Dutch 2.

The Lord's Prayer, as spoken at the present time.

Guthrie, p. 728.

EGYPTIAN 1.

a b c d e f g h

i k l m n o p q

r s t v x y z th

EGYPTIAN 2.

a b c d e f g h

i k l m n o p q

r s t v x y z th

EGYPTIAN 3.

a b c d e f g h

i k l m n o p q

r s t u x y z

EGYPTIAN 1.

The Egyptians, before their knowledge of letters and characters, expressed their thoughts by the representation of the forms of various animals, trees, plants, herbs, and even of several of their own members, which they called Hieroglyphic. They had also letters which were used by the Ethiopians, approaching to the Hebrew, but we have no certainty as to their language or writing.

Theseus Ambrosius, in his "Appendice des langues "Chaldaique, Syriaque, et Armenienne," gives this as the most ancient Egyptian.

Duret, p. 380.

EGYPTIAN 2.

This is given, on the authority of Theseus, as the second Egyptian alphabet.

Duret, p. 381.

EGYPTIAN 3.

Fournier calls this *Isiac-Egyptien*, which, he informs us, is attributed to Isis, the Egyptian Goddess.

Vol. 2. p. 273.

Egyptian 4.

a b c d e f g h

i k l m n o p q

r s t u x y z

Egyptian 5.

a b c d e f g h

i k l m n o p q

r s t v x y z z

Egyptian 6.

a a b d h v z hh

i k l m n s aa q

q r sh t

EGYPTIAN 4.

Fournier calls this *Lettres Sacrées*, and says they are attributed to the Mercury Thot.

Vol. 2. p. 273.

EGYPTIAN 5.

This alphabet has generally been received as hieroglyphic, according to Ambrosius, but there does not appear sufficient reason for it.

Duret, p. 382.
Fourn. v. 2. p. 273.

EGYPTIAN 6.

This alphabet was discovered by the late Abbé Barthelemi, from whose sagacity and enquiries there can be no doubt of it's being Egyptian; and being found under a monument in Egypt, had never been decyphered before.

Encyc. Franc. pl. 5.

EGYPTIAN 7.

EGYPTIAN 8.

NEW ENGLAND.

Nooshun kesukquot, quittiana tamunach koo wesuonk; peyaumooutch kukketassootamoonk, kuttenantamoonk, nen nach ohkeit nean kesukqut; nummeet uongash asekesukokish, assamatineau yeuyeu kesukod; kah ahquontamatinneau numat cheseongash, neane matchenehu queagig nuta quontamounnonog;

EGYPTIAN 7.

This character is different from every other of this name, being written from right to left.

Fourn. v. 2. p. 273.

EGYPTIAN 8.

Remarkable hieroglyphics engraved on the chair of a colossal statue near LUXXOR and CARNAC.

Norden's Antiquities of Egypt and Nubia, v. 2. p. 111.

NEW ENGLAND.

The Lord's Prayer.

Wilk. Ess. p. 435.

English.

There is not, perhaps, any language in the world, which has experienced so many revolutions as this; and, like the political constitution of the country, it seems to have gained both strength and energy by every change.

We may conclude, from Cæsar's account of this island, and it's inhabitants, that about the beginning of the Christian Æra, the language of the ancient Britons was the same, or very similar, to that of Gaul, or France, at that time, and which is now believed to have been the parent of the Celtic, Erse, Gaelic, or Welch; for the intercourse between this island and Gaul, in Cæsar's time, as well as their relative situations, render it more than probable, that Britain was peopled from that part of the continent, as both Cæsar and Tacitus affirm and prove, by many strong and conclusive arguments.

There are now but few remains of the ancient British tongue, except in Wales, Cornwall, the Isles and Highlands of Scotland, part of Ireland, and some provinces of France; which will not appear strange, when we consider that Julius Cæsar, some time before the birth of our Saviour, made a descent on Britain; and in the time of Claudius, about A. D. 45, Aulus Plautius was sent over with some Roman forces, who overcame the two kings of the Britons, Togodumnus and Charactacus, when the southern parts of the island were reduced to the form of a Roman province; after which, Agricola subdued the island, as far as Scotland; whereupon a great number of the Britons retired into Wales, Scotland, and the Isles, carrying their language with them. The greatest part of Britain being thus become a Roman province, the Legions who resided in the island above 200 years, undoubtedly disseminated the Latin tongue; and the people being afterwards governed by laws written in Latin, must necessarily create a mixture of languages.

English.

Thus the British tongue continued, for some time, mixed with the provincial Latin, 'till the Roman Legions being called home, the Scots and Picts took the opportunity to attack and harrass England: upon which, Vortigern about 440, called the Saxons to his assistance, for which he rewarded them with the Isle of Thanet, and the whole County of Kent; but they growing powerful, and discontented, dispossessed the inhabitants of all the country eastward of the Severn; by which means the Saxon language was introduced.

In the beginning of the 9th century, the Danes invaded England, and became sole masters of it in about 200 years, whereby the British language obtained a tincture of the Danish; but this did not make so great an alteration in the Anglo-Saxon, as the revolution in 1066 by William the First, who, as a monument of the Norman conquest, and in imitation of other conquerors, endeavoured to make the language of his own country as generally received as his commands; thus the ancient English became an entire medley of Celtic, Latin, Saxon, Danish, and Norman-French.

Since the restoration of learning, the sciences have been cultivated with such success in this island, that in astronomy, anatomy, natural history, natural philosophy, chemistry, medicine, and the fine arts, innumerable terms have been borrowed from that inexhaustible source, the Greek. Italy, Spain, Holland, and Germany, have also contributed something, so that the present English may be considered as a selection from all the languages of Europe.

The alphabets now in use will be found under the articles Roman and Italic.

English 1.

On ðære tide þe Gotan of Siððiu mægþe
ƿiþ Romana rice geƿin upahofon. ⁊ miþ heora cẏningum. Rædgota and Eallerica ƿæ-
ron hotne. Romane burig abræcon. ⁊ eall
Italia rice ꝥ is betƿux þam muntum ⁊ Sici-
lia ðam ealonde in anƿald gerehton. ⁊ þa
æfter þam foresprecenan cẏningum Ðeodric feng to þam ilcan rice. se Ðeodric
ƿæs Amulinga. he ƿæs Cristen. þeah he on
þan Arrianiscan gedƿolan ðurhƿunode. He
gehet Romanum his freondscipe. sƿa ꝥ hi
mortan heora ealdrihta ƿẏrðe beon. Ac
he þa gehat sƿiðe ẏfele gelæste. ⁊ sƿiðe

English 2.

Ðis gære for þe king Stephne ofer sæ to
Normandi. ⁊ þer ƿes under-fangen. forði
ꝥ hi ƿenden ꝥ he sculde ben alsuic alse þe
eom ƿes. ⁊ for he hadde get his tresor.
ac he to-deld it ⁊ scatered sotlice. Micel
hadde Henri king gadered gold ⁊ sẏluer.
and na god ne dide me for his saule þar
of. Ða þe king Stephne to Engla land com
þa macod he his gadering æt Oxene-ford.
⁊ þar he nam þe biscop Roger of Seres-
beri. ⁊ Alexander biscop of Lincoln. ⁊ te
Canceler Roger hise neues. ⁊ dide ælle in

English 1.

Doctor Johnson, in his history of the English language, being the preface to his Quarto Dictionary, 1785, gives the annexed as the earliest specimen of it, taken from King Alfred's Paraphrase, or imitation of Boethius, which is here given in the Saxon character as used at that time.

See Saxon.

English 2.

About 1150, in the reign of King Stephen, according to Dr. Johnson, the Saxon language began to take the form in which the present English was plainly discovered. The specimen I have given is extracted from Gibson's Saxon Chronicle, of the date of 1137, p. 238.

English 3.

Ure fadyr in heaven rich,
Thy name be hallyed ever lich,
Thou bring us thy michell blisse:
Als hit in heaven y doe,
Evar in yearth beene it also.
That holy bread that lasteth ay,
Thou send it ous this ilke day,
Forgive ous all that we have don,
As we forgivet uch other mon:
Ne let ous fall into no founding,
Ac shield ous fro the fowle thing. Amen.

English 4.

Fadir ur that es in hevene,
Halud be thi Nam to nevene:
Thou do us thi rich rike,
Thi Will erd be wroght elk:
As it is wroght in Heven ay,
Ur ilk Day Brede give us to Day:
Forgive thou all us dettes urs
As we forgive till ur detturs
And ledde us in na fanding
But sculd us fra ivel Thing.

English 3.

About 1160, in the reign of King Henry II. the annexed Lord's Prayer was rendered in rhyme, and sent from Rome by Pope Adrian, an Englishman.

Wilk. Ess. p. 7.
Orat. Dom. p. 68.

English 4.

About 1250, in the reign of Henry III. we find it thus rendered also in rhyme.

Martin's Inst. p. 15.

English 5.

Fader that art in heavin riche,
Thin helge nam it wurth the blisse,
Cumen and mot thy kingdom,
Thin holy will it bẹ all don,
In heaven and in erdh also,
So it shall bin full well Ic tro.
Gif us all bread on this day,
And forgif us ure sinnes,
As we do ure wider winnes:
Let us not in fonding fall,
Oac fro evil thu syld us all. Amen.

English 6.

Oure Fadir that art in Hevenes, halowid be thi Name. Thi Kingdom come to. Be thi Will doon in erthe as in hevene: Geve to us this dai our breed over othir Substance. And forgeve to us our dettis as we forgeven to our dettouris. And lede us not into Temptacionn but deliver us from yvel. Amen.

English 5.

In the year 1260, in the reign of King Henry III. the annexed translation of the Lord's Prayer is also given in rhyme.

Wilk. Ess. p. 7.

English 6.

This specimen of the gradual improvement of our language, is handed to us from Wickliffe's translation of the New Testament in the year 1380, and in the reign of Richard II.

Martin's Inst. p. 15.

English 7.

Oure Fadir that art in Hevenes, halewid be thi Name, thi Kingdom com to thee, be thi will don in Eerthe as in Hevene, give to us this Day oure Breed over othre Substanc; and forgive to us oure Dettis, as we forgiven oure Dettouris, and lede us not into Temptation, but deliver us from ivel. Amen.

English 8.

Our Father which art in Heven, halowed be thy Name. Let thy Kingdom come; thy will be fulfilled as well in Earth as it is in Heven. Geve us this daye in dayly bred; and forgeve us oure detters. And leade us not into Temptation; but delyver us from evyll. For thyne is the Kyngdom, and the power and the glorye for ever. Amen.

English 9.

O oure Father which arte in heven halowed be thy name. Let thy kingdome come. Thy will be fulfilled, as well in erth, as it is in heven. Geve us this daye oure dayly bred. And forgeve us our treaspases, even as we forgeve oure trespacers. And lead us not into temptacion, but delyver us from evyll. Amen.

English 7.

About the year 1430, in the reign of Henry VI. as appears by a large MS. vellum Bible in the Oxford Library, which was given by this King to the Carthusians, at London, the Lord's Prayer was thus rendered.

Wilk. Ess. p. 8.

English 8.

We find the first version of the Lord's Prayer, with the doxology, in Tyndale's translation, in the year 1526, in the reign of Henry VIII.

Martin's Inst. p. 16.

English 9.

About ten years after, and in the same reign, we meet with another Bible, set forth by the King's license, and translated by Thomas Mathew, in which the Lord's Prayer is thus differently given.

Wilk. Ess. p. 8.

ENGLISH 10.

Our father which art in heaven, halowed be thy name, Let thy Kingdom come, Thy will be fulfilled, as well in earth as it is in heaven: Give ous this day our dayly bread: And forgive ous our trespasses, even as we forgive our trespassers: And lead ous not into temptation, But delyver ous from evyl. Amen.

ENGLISH 11.

O our father which art in heauen halowed be thy name. Let thy kingdome come. Thy wyll be done, as well in earth, as it is in heauen. Give vs this Day our dayly breade. And forgyue vs our dettes, as we forgyue our detters. And leade vs not into temptation, but deliuer vs from euill: for thine is the kingdome, and the power, and the glorie, for euer. Amen.

ENGLISH 12.

Our Father which art in Heaven hallowed bee thy Name. Thy Kingdom come. Thy Will bee done even in Earth as it is in Heaven. Give us this Day our daily Bread and forgive us our Dettes, as wee also forgive our Detters. And leade us not into Temptation but deliver us from evil: for thine is the Kingdom, and the Power and the Glory for ever. Amen.

English 10.

This version is handed to us as a translation by Sir John Cheke, Professor of Greek in the University of Cambridge, in the reign of Edward VI.

Orat. Dom. p. 69.

English 11.

The annexed Lord's Prayer is taken from Archbishop Cranmer's Bible, in the author's possession, which was printed in 1575, in the reign of Queen Elizabeth.

English 12.

In 1610, in the time of James I. we find it in a Bible, printed at London by Barker, rendered thus.

Martin's Inst. p. 16.

ENGLISH 13.

Our Father who art in Heaven, sacredly reverenced be thy Name; Let thy Kingdom come; may thy Will be done, even on Earth according as in Heaven; Give us our daily bread to day; and forgive us our trespasses, as we also forgive those that trespass against us; and do not bring us into trial, but deliver us from wickedness; since the Kingdom, Power and Glory is thine for ever: so let it be.

ENGLISH 14.

Our father which art in heaven, hallowed be thy Name; thy kingdom come; thy will be done in earth as it is in heaven; give us this day our daily bread; and forgive us our debts as we forgive our debtors: and lead us not into temptation, but deliver us from evil: for thine is the kingdom and the power and the glory for ever. Amen.

ENGLISH 15.

𝔄𝔞 𝔅𝔟 ℭ𝔠 𝔇𝔡 𝔈𝔢 𝔉𝔣 𝔊𝔤 ℌ𝔥

ℑ𝔦𝔧 𝔎𝔨 𝔏𝔩 𝔐𝔪 𝔑𝔫 𝔒𝔬 𝔓𝔭 𝔔𝔮

ℜ𝔯 𝔖𝔰 𝔗𝔱 𝔘𝔲 𝔚𝔴 𝔛𝔵 𝔜𝔶 ℨ𝔷

English 13.

The annexed reading of the Lord's Prayer is taken from Anthony Purver's new and literal translation of the Old and New Testament, published in 1764, corrected by himself. Matth. VI. v. 9, &c.

English 14.

This is the modern reading of the Lord's Prayer, as given in the Bibles and Testaments now published in our Universities, taken from the Gofpel of St. Matthew, chap. VI. v. 9, &c.

English 15.

This character, which is derived from the Gothic, is called by the French *Lettres de forme;* by us it is known under the name of Old English, or *Black Letter:* it was the first used by Guttemberg and Faust at Mentz, and was by them and the printers denominated *Lettres Bourgeoises.*

English 16.

AaBbCcDdEeFfff

GgHhIiijKkLlllMm

NnOoPpQqRrꝛS

ſsTtVuvWwXxYyZz.

English 17.

Aa Bbb Ccc Ddd Eeee

ffff Ggg hhh Iij kk Lll m

Nn Oo o o Ppp Qqs Rr

ꝛ Ss ſ & tt Uu W xyz.

English 16.

Set Chancery. This alphabet began to take place in this country about the decline of the fourteenth century, and is, with the following, or *Running Chancery*, used in the enrollments of letters patent, charters, &c. and in the exemplification of recoveries.

Astle on Writing, p. 145.

English 17.

Running Chancery.

See the above note.

English 18.

A B C D E F G H

I K L M N O P Q

R S T V W Y Z

English 19.

A B C D E F G H

I K L M N O P Q

R S T V W Y Z

English 20.

a b c d e f g h

i k l m n o p q

r s t v w x y z

English 18.

Court or *Exchequer Text.* The Court of Exchequer was erected by William the Conqueror, it's model being taken from a similar one established in Normandy long before his time.

These characters were invented by the English lawyers about 1550, and continued in use 'till the beginning of the late reign, when it was abolished by act of Parliament.

Astle on Writing, p. 145.

English 19.

The lower case or small letters corresponding with the above.

English 20.

Church Text. As the lawyers had alphabets appropriated to various purposes, it seemed reasonable that Ecclesiastics should not be behind in invention, especially as they were esteemed the curators of all learning for five centuries; they therefore invented this alphabet for the use of the church.

English 21.

And whereas by Indenture
of aſsignment bearing date
on or about the sixth day of
June in the Year of our Lord
one thouſand seven hundred
and eighty seven made be
tween the said Edmund Fry
of London of the one and

Ecclemach.

A friend	*Nigefech*	A bow	*Pagounach*
The beard	*Iscotre*	To dance	*Mefpa*
The teeth	*Aour*	Seal	*Opobabos*
No	*Maal*	Yes	*Ike*
Father	*Aoi*	Mother	*Atzia*
Star	*Aimoulas*	Night	*Toumanes*
One	*Pek*	Six	*Pekoulana*
Two	*Oulach*	Seven	*Houlakoala*
Three	*Oullef*	Eight	*Koulefala*
Four	*Amnahou*	Nine	*Kamakoual*
Five	*Pemaka*	Ten	*Tomoïla*

English 21.

Secretary; invented in the 16th century, and has been used ever since by English lawyers, in engrossing their conveyances and legal instruments.

Astle on Writing, p. 146.

Ecclemach.

This is the language of a colony of North California, which differs widely from those of all their neighbours, and possesses more resemblance to our European tongues, than to those of North America.

The specimen given is extracted from the vocabulary.

Pérouse, Vol. 2. p. 245.

Esquimaux.

The hair	*New-rock*	The eye	*Ehich*
Eye-brow	*Coop-loot*	The nose	*Cring-yauk*
The ear	*Se-u-teck*	The chin	*Taplow*
The neck	*Coon-e-soke*	The arm	*Telluk*
The hand	*Alguit*	The leg	*Ki-naw-auk*
The foot	*E-te-ket*	The sun	*Suek-ki-nuc*
The moon	*Tac-cock*	Fire	*Ekoma*
A house	*Tope-uck*	A canoe	*Kirock*
A paddle	*Pow*	Iron	*Shaveck*
The breast	*Suck-ke-uc*	Arrows	*Caucjuck*
One	*Attouset*	Six	*Arbanget*
Two	*Mardluk*	Seven	*Attausek*
Three	*Pingasut*	Eight	*Mardlik*
Four	*Sissamat*	Nine	*Kollin illoe*
Five	*Tellimat*	Ten	*Kollit*

Esthonic.

Issa meddi ke sinna ollet Taiwas, pohitzetut sakut sunno nimmi. Tulckut meile sunno rickus. Sunno tachtminne sundkut, kui Taiwas, ninda kahs mah pehl. Meddi iggapeiwase leiba anna meile tennapeiw. Nink anna meile andix meddi wolgkat, kudt meie andix anname meddi wolgkaleisille. Nink erra satameid kinsatusse sisze. Erranis erhapehsta meid keickest kurjast. Sest sunno on se rickus, nink se weggi, nink se auw, iggawest. Amen.

Esquimaux.

The Esquimaux inhabit that vast tract of country called Labrador, or New Britain, in North America. The specimen given is taken from the vocabulary of the language.

Cook's Last Voy. v. 3. p. 554.

Esthonic.

Esthonia is a Russian government, on the east of the Baltic. The specimen given is the Lord's Prayer.

Orat. Dom. p. 43.

Ethiopic 1.

አቡነ፡ ዘበሰማያት፡ ይትቀደስ፡ ስምብ፡፡ ትምጻእ፡ መንግ
ሠትከ፡፡ ይኩን፡ ፍቃከ፡ በከመ፡ በሰማይ፡ ወበምድርኒ፡፡
ሲሳየነ፡ ዘለለ፡ ዕለትነ፡ ሀበነ፡ ዮም፡፡ ኅድግ፡ ለነ፡ አበሰነ፡
ከመ፡ ንሐነኒ፡ ንኅድግ፡ ለዘ፡ አበሰ፡ ለነ፡፡ ወሊቲብአነ፡
ውስተ፡ መንሲት፡፡ አሳ፡ አድኅነነ፡ ወባልሐነ፡ አምኰሉ፡
እኩይ፡፡ እስመ፡ ዚአከ፡ ይእቲ፡ መንግሠት፡ ኃይል፡ ወስብ
ሐት፡ ለዓለመ፡ ዓለም፡ አሜን፡፡ አቡነ፡ ዘበሰማያት፡ ይ
ትቀደስ፡ ስምብ፡፡ ትምጻእ፡ መንግሠታከ፡፡ ይኩን፡ ፍቃደ

Ethiopic 2.

Abuna xabashamajath. Yithkadash shimacha Thymtsa mangystcha. Yichun phachadacha. Bachama bashamai wabamdyrni. Shishajana zalala ylathana habana yom. Hydyglana aba shana. Chama nyhhnani nyhadyg laxa abasha lana. Waithabyana wysh tha manshuthi, ala adychnana balhhanana ymkulu ychui.

Etruscan 1.

a b g d ĕ f z ē

th i k l m n ŏ p

r s t ph ps

ETHIOPIC 1.

Called also AMHARIC, from Amhara, the chief city of Abyssinia. The dialects of this language vary in the different provinces subject to Ethiopia; but the same character or letter, which Bruce calls the GEEZ, is used to express the several tongues of AMHARA, GEEZ, FALASHA, GALLA, DAMOT AGOW, TCHERATZ AGOW, and GAFAT; and that it was invented by a Cushite shepherd.

Bruce, vol. 1. p 401.

The specimen given is the Lord's Prayer in the Ethiopic character.

Orat. Dom. p. 14.

ETHIOPIC 2.

This is a literal reading of the above.

Wilk. Ess. p. 435.

ETRUSCAN 1.

The Etruscans, or Etrurians, as Latin history informs us, were the most ancient people of Italy. Some authors assert, that, soon after the universal deluge, Noah established there twelve cities, or tribes, who used the same letters or characters, which were entrusted to the priests alone, who varied them according to their pleasure, as to their order, and value or import; writing them sometimes from left to right, or the reverse. There is no doubt but the Etruscan and Pelasgic alphabets, (which see,) are to be traced to the same origin. See Astle on these alphabets.

The specimen given is copied from the Encyc. Franc. pl. VIII.

Duret, p. 757.

Etruscan 2.

a	b	c	d	e	f	g	h
i	k	l	m	n	o	p	q
r	s	t	u	x	y		

Etruscan 3.

h	g	f	e	d	c	b	a
q	p	o	n	m	l	k	i
il	ch	z	x	v	t	s	

Finland.

Isa meiden joca olet taivvaisa, pyhittetty stolcon sinum nymes; la he stolcon sinum vvaldacunda, olcon sinum tahtos nyen maasa cujnon taivvas, anna meille tana paivvan; meiden jo capaivvainen leipam: Ia anna meidan vvelcamme andexi, ninquin me andexi annamme meiden vvelgolisten, ja ala johdata mei ta kin sauxen; mutta paasta meita paastha, silla

ETRUSCAN 2.

This character, which is written from left to right, Theseus Ambrosius says, is to be found in many libraries in Italy.

Duret, p. 757.
Le Clabart, p. 624.

ETRUSCAN 3.

On the above authority we have also this character, which is written from right to left.

Duret, p. 758.
Le Clabart, p. 623.

FINLAND.

The Sclavon tongue was formerly used in this country, but since it came under the dominion of the kings of Sweden, they have spoken two languages; the Sclavon in one part, and the Swedish in another; but in the interior of the country, they have a proper one, of which the annexed is the Lord's Prayer.

Duret, p. 868.
Orat. Dom. p. 44.

Flemish.

Aa Bb Cc Dd Ee Ff Gg Hh Ii ij ÿ

Kk Ll Mm Nn Oo Pp Qq Rr ꝛ

Sſ ß Tt Uu Vv w Xx Yy Zz Et œ &

Formosan.

Diameta ka tu vullum lulugniang ta nanang oho, maba tongal ta tao tu goumoho, mamtalto ki kamoienhu tu nai mama tu vullum: pecame ka cangniang wagi katta. Hamiecame ki váraviang mamemiang mamia ta varau ki tao ka mouro ki riich emitang. Inecame poudangadangach souaia mecame ki litto, ka imhouato ta gumaguma kallipuchang kasasamagang, mikaqua. Amen.

Franco-Gallic.

ꞇ	b	c	ꝺ	e	ꝼ	ᵹ	h
a	b	c	d	e	f	g	h
ı	L	m	n	o	p	q	ꞃ
i	l	m	n	o	p	q	r
	s	τ	u	x	y	z	
	s	t	u	x	y	z	

Flemish.

This is the proper character of the Austrian and French Netherlands, and is used in their common printing.

Formosan.

This is the Lord's Prayer, in the native language of this island.

Orat. Dom. p. 62.

Franco-Gallic.

This character was used under the first race of the kings of France, in their public acts. It was so named, because the French mixed their letters with those of the Gauls, whom they had conquered.

Fourn. v. 2. p. 270.

Franks 1.

a b c d e f g h

i k l m n ŏ p r

s t x y ph ch ps ō

Franks 2.

a b c d e f g h

i k l m n o p q

r s t u x y

French 1.

a b c d e f g h

i k l m n o p q

r s t u x y

Franks 1.

The Franks, who survived the destruction of Troy about 1140, B. C. came and settled in the low countries of Germany, under Marcomin their leader, where the Saxons afforded them an asylum near the mouths of the Rhine; whence, after some time, they made frequent and vigorous attacks upon their neighbours, and were in continual wars against the Romans and Gauls upwards of 900 years; and extended their empire over great part of Europe, according to Hunibauld, who informs us, that Vuastbal wrote in this character an account of their conquests, and every thing remarkable during 758 years. This alphabet is also given on the authority of the Abbé Triteme.

Duret, p. 865.

Franks 2.

The language of this people, called Lingua Franca, is a kind of jargon spoken on the Mediterranean, particularly the coasts of the Levant, composed of Italian, Spanish, French, vulgar Greek, and other tongues.

Massey, p. 103.

French 1.

This alphabet was used in France in the fifth century, under the first race of their kings.

Fourn. v. 2. p. 268.

French 2.

Nostre pere qui es és cieulx, ton nom soit santifie; ton royaume advenie; ta volonte soit facte, ainsi en la terre comme au cieulx; nostre pain quotidiain donne nous aviourdhuy; et pardonne nous noz faultes, comme nous pardonnons a ceulx qui nous ont offenzes; et ne nous induy point en tentation, mais deliure nous de mal. Amen.

French 3.

Notre Père qui es aux cieux, ton nom soit sanctifié. Ton règne vienne. Ta volonté soit faite en la terre comme au ciel. Donne-nous aujourd'hui notre pain quotidien. Pardonne-nous nos offenses, comme nous pardonnons à ceux qui nous ont offensés. Et ne nous induis point en la tentation, mais nous délivre de mal. Amen.

Frisic.

Ws Haita duu derstu biste yne hymil, dyn name wird heiligt, dyn ryck tokomme, dyn wille moet schoen, opt yrtryck as yne hymil. Ws deilix bræ jov ws juved; in verjou ws, vvs schylden, as wy vejac ws schyldnirs; In lied ws nact in versieking: Din fry ws vin it quæd: Dan dyn is it ryck, de macht,

French 2.

The Lord's Prayer.

Wilk. Ess. p. 435.

French 3.

The Lord's Prayer in the language as spoken at this day.

Guthrie, p. 849.

Frisic.

The Lord's Prayer.

Wilk. Ess. p. 435.

Friendly Isles.

Ve faine	*A woman*	Maiee	*Bread fruit*
Koeea	*Yes*	Fooroo	*The hair*
Fooee vy	*The leg*	Eboore	*The breast*
Etooa	*The back*	Elelo	*The tongue*
Etarre	*To cough*	Hengatoo	*Cloth*
Efangoo	*To sneeze*	Moe	*Sleep*
Tangooroo	*To snore*	Ekatta	*To laugh*
Etolle	*A hatchet*	Aiee	*A fan*
Enoo	*A belt*	Etovee	*A club*
Eao	*A hat*	Poooree	*Night*
Fooo	*A nail*	Epallo	*A rat*
Matangee	*Wind*	Tamadje	*A child*
Elango	*A fly*	Efonno	*A turtle*
Kaee	*No*	Moeha	*More*
Veenaga	*Charming*	Totto	*Blood*
Eeegee	*A chief*	Eatooa	*God*
Elangee	*The sky*	Elaa	*The sun*
Ao	*Clouds*	Laa	*A sail*

Friulian.

Pari nestri ch'ees in cijl, see sanctificaat la to nom; vigna lu to ream, see fatta la too voluntaat, sice' in cijl, et in tierra: Da nus hu'-el nestri pan cotidian; et perdonni nus glu nestris debiz, sicu noo perduin agl nestris debetoors. E no nus menaa in tentation; mà libora nus dal mal. Amen.

Friendly Isles.

These are a cluster of islands in the South Pacific Ocean, and were so named by Capt. James Cook in 1773; they are situated between 20 and 23 degrees of south latitude, and between 170 and 180 degrees of west longitude.

This specimen of the language is taken from the vocabulary.

Cook's Voy. Vol. 3. p. 531.

Friulian.

Or *Forojulian;* this specimen of the language is the Lord's Prayer.

Wilk. Ess. p. 435.

Gambia.

Killing	*One*	Sae	*Eight*
Foola	*Two*	Conunte	*Nine*
Saba	*Three*	Tang	*Ten*
Nane	*Four*	Tangkillin	*Eleven*
Looloo	*Five*	Emva	*Twenty*

Georgian 1.

Georgian 2.

a b gh d e v sz h th i

ch l m n i o p sg r s

t v f k ghh cq sc c zz z

zz cc chh hh g hha hho

Gambia.

Taken from the vocabulary of numeration of the negroes on the river Gambia in Africa; but no mention is made of their peculiar language.

Park. Voy. p. 206.

Georgian 1.

This alphabet is formed from the Greek, according to Postellus, who says, that the Georgians use that language in their prayers, but on other occasions they employ the Tartarian and Armenian letters. This specimen is almost Greek, both by name and figure, and was taken from an ancient book of voyages to the Holy Land, by a Monk named Nicolle Huès, A. D. 1487.

Duret, p. 749.
Fourn. v. 2. p. 221.

Georgian 2.

This, and the two succeeding alphabets, according to the Encyc. Franc. are in use among the Georgians, and are written from left to right; but Fournier says, that the name is taken from the Martyr St. George, whom the Iberians have chosen for their patron, and regard as their Apostle.

The alphabets, of which these are only the capital letters, are called *sacred*, from their having been used in transcribing their Holy Books.

Fourn. v. 2. p. 276.
Encyc. Franc. pl. XIV.

Georgian 3.

a	b	gh	d	e	v	sz	h	th	i
ch	l	m	n	i	o	p	sg	r	s
t	v	f	k	ghh	cq	sc	c	zz	z
zz	cc	chh	hh	g	hha	hho			

Georgian 4.

a	b	gh	d	e	v	sz	h	th	i
ch	l	m	n	i	o	p	sg	r	s
t	v	f	k	ghh	cq	sc	c	zz	z
zz	cc	chh	hh	g	hha	hho			

Georgian 3.

This alphabet is only the small or lower case letters to the former.

Fourn. v. 2. p. 276.
Encyc. Franc. pl. XIV.

Georgian 4.

This is the cursive, or common running hand of the Georgians, and is in use at the present time.

Encyc. Franc. pl. XIV.
Fourn. v. 2. p. 276.

Georgian 5.

Mamao cjueno romeli chbar zzahta sciua. Tzmida ikachn sa-chheli sceni. Sceni movedin suphocha sceni. Ikachn neba sceni os zatha scina eghre kue-chanisa szeda. Puri cjueni arsobisa momez cjuens dges da. Momitheven cjuenthana nadebni cjueni os cjuen miutevebth thana mjebtha math cjuentha. Ala michsneb cjuen borothifagan. Amin.

German 1.

A B C D E F G H

I K L M N O P Q

R S T V W X Y Z

German 2.

a b c d e f g h

i j k l m n o p q

r ꝛ ſ s t u v x y z

GEORGIAN 5.

The literal reading of the Lord's Prayer.

Orat. Dom. p. 31.

GERMAN 1.

A specimen of this language is already given under the article HIGH DUTCH, (which see). This alphabet shews the capital letters in use for their general printing.

Fourn. v. 2. p. 267.
Encyc. Franc. pl. X.

GERMAN 2.

These are the lower case or small letters to the above.

Fourn. v. 2. p. 267.
Encyc. Franc. pl. X.

Gothic 1.

Gothic 2.

a b g d e f g h

th i k l m n o p

q r s t u w x y z

Gothic 3.

a b c d e f g h

i k l m n o p q

r s t v w x y z

GOTHIC.

In the history of the North, we are informed that Ulphilas, or Gulphila, bishop of the Goths, who lived in Mæsia about A. D. 370, was the first who invented the letters or characters of his nation; and that he translated the holy scriptures out of the Greek into his proper language. Jean le Grand gives him full credit for the latter, but insists that the letters were in use before the bishop's time. Other historians assert, that the Goths always had the use of letters, and what confirms this sentiment is, that Le Grand, in his history of Gothic characters, says, that before, or very soon after the flood, there were found, engraved in letters on large stones, the memorable acts of great men.

Olaus Magnus, brother to Le Grand, assures us, that the Goths wrote upon wood, and upon the bark of trees, worked into sheets, and sometimes on skins; and that they used ink made of coal finely ground, with milk or water.

It is asserted by different authors, that they wrote the Celtic and Teutonic.

Duret, p. 862.
Olaus Mag. p. 14.

GOTHIC 1.

This is given as the earliest Gothic, and seems to have great affinity to the Runic,

Fourn. v. 2. p. 271.
Duret, p. 862.
Le Clabart, p. 379.

GOTHIC 2.

This character, which is formed of the Greek and Latin, is attributed to Ulphilas, bishop of the Goths above mentioned, who is said to have invented them about A. D. 388.

Spanh. Dissert. p. 114.
Dr. Morton's Tables.
Massey, p. 103.

GOTHIC 3.

This alphabet, which is much like the German, has been a long time in use in France: It is attributed to Albert Durer, who flourished early in the sixteenth century.

Encyc. Franc. pl. IX.

Gothic 4.

Atta unsar thu in himinam; veihnai namo thein; Quimai thiudinassus theins, vairthai vilja theins, sve in himina, jah ana airthai. Hlaif unsarana thana sinteinan gif uns himmadaga. Jah aflet uns thatei sculans sijaima sua sue jah veis afletam thaim skulam unsaraim; jah ni briggais uns in fraistubnjai. Ak lausei uns af thamma ubilin. Amen.

Mæso Gothic.

𐌰	𐌱	𐌲	𐌳	𐌴	𐍆	𐌾	𐌷
a	b	g	d	e	f	gj	h
𐌹	𐌺	𐌻	𐌼	𐌽	𐍉	𐍀	𐍈
i	k	l	m	n	o	p	hp
𐍂	𐍃	𐍄	𐌸	𐌵	𐍅	𐍇	𐌶
r	s	t	th	q	w	ch	z

Grandan.

ă	ĭ	oŭ	roŭ	loŭ	e	o	am
kha	gha	tcha	ja	jha	igna	ta	tha
dạ	na	pa	ba	ya	ra	la	va

Gothic 4.

This is the literal reading of the Lord's Prayer.

Orat. Dom. p. 21.
Wilk. Ess. p. 435.

Mæso Gothic.

This letter is also attributed to Ulphilas, and was used in the translation of the holy scriptures.

Encyc. Franc. pl. IX.
Fourn. v. 2. p. 271.

Grandan.

An Indian alphabet, said to be in use at Pondicherry, but it seems to be incomplete.

Encyc. Franc. pl. XVI.

Greenland.

Angut	*A man*	Iglo	*A house*
Kaiak	*A canoe*	Pautik	*A paddle*
Aglikak	*Darts*	Nag	*No*
Illisve	*Yes*	Attousek	*One*
Arlak	*Two*	Pingajuah	*Three*
Sissamat	*Four*	Tellimat	*Five*

Grisons.

Bab nos quel tii ist in eschil, santifichio saia ilgtes num; ilgtes ariginam uigna ter nus, la thia uoeglia d'uainta, in terra sco la fo in eschil; do a nus nos paun houtz & in miinchia di; parduna à nus nos dbits, sco nus fain à nos dbitaduors; nun ens mener in mel aprouaimaint; dimpersemaing spendra nus da tuots mels. Amen.

Guelderland.

Onse Vayer, die ghey seit in den hemel; geheylicht sey uwen naem; wu reyck ons toecoem, uwen will geschieh up erden, als in de hemel; geeft ons heuyen ons daghelichs broot: ende vergeeft ons onse sculdt, als wey vergeven onse sculdengers; ende enleyt ons met in becooringhe; sondern verloest ons van allen quaden. Amen.

GREENLAND.

Taken from the table, shewing the affinity between the languages spoken at OONALASHKA and NORTON SOUND, and those of the GREENLANDERS and ESQUIMAUX.

Cook's Voy. Vol. 3. p. 554.

GRISONS.

A small republic of Italy, inhabiting the Alps.
This specimen of their language is the Lord's Prayer.

Wilk. Ess. p. 435.

GUELDERLAND.

This is also the Lord's Prayer.

Orat. Dom. p. 56.

Greek.

The alphabets given under this title were those originally in use over all Europe. Even those countries which did not speak the Greek language, employed the characters of it. Cæsar found them in use among the ancient Gauls, and there can be no doubt but the Roman language and characters were derived from the same sources as the Greek.

Before the victories of Alexander, this language was principally confined to Turkey in Europe, Sicily, Dalmatia, Anatolia, and the islands of the Archipelago; his generals and successors extended it over many parts of Asia and Egypt; so that from the time of Alexander, to that of Pompey, it may be considered as having been the most general language of the world; and what is truly astonishing, it continues to be spoken in a manner, which would have been intelligible to the ancient inhabitants of Greece.

This is, perhaps, an instance of the greatest longevity of language; few others having continued living and intelligible more than 500, whereas the Greek has survived 3500 years.

The causes of this will be found in the structure of the language itself, the extent of it's use, and the great merit of the authors who have written in it; as historians, orators, poets, philosophers, mathematicians, and theologians: the New Testament, as well as the early fathers, are also written in Greek.

In this, the terms of art are very significant, which is the reason that modern languages borrow so many technical terms from it. When any new invention, instrument, machine, &c. is discovered, recourse is generally had to the Greek for a name, the facility with which words are compounded, affording such as are expressive of it's use; viz. Pantographia, music, barometer, eidouranion, philosophy, &c. &c.

GREEK.

Besides the copiousness and significancy of this language, wherein it excels most, if not all, others, it has three numbers, viz. a singular, dual, and plural; also abundance of tenses in it's verbs, making a variety in discourse, and prevents that dryness always accompanying too great an uniformity, and renders it peculiarly proper for all kinds of poetry.

It is not an easy matter to assign the precise interval between the modern and ancient Greek, which is to be distinguished by the terminations of the nouns, pronouns, verbs, &c. not unlike what obtains between some of the dialects of the Italian and Spanish.

There are also, in the modern Greek, many new words, not to be met with in the ancient: we may therefore distinguish three ages of this tongue, the first of which ends at the time when Constantinople became the capital of the Roman empire, about A. D. 360; from which period the second continued 'till the taking of that city by the Turks, in 1453; and the third from that to the present time.

When we compare the ancient Greek with the Phenician and Samaritan alphabets, no doubt can remain of their origin; and it is probable, that the use of letters travelled, progressively, from Chaldea to Phenicia, and thence along the coast of the Mediterranean, to Crete and Ionia, whence it might readily have passed over into Greece.

As Inachus and Cecrops were said to have been Egyptians, as was Agenor, the father of Cadmus, some have supposed that the Greeks received their alphabet from Egypt: if this be true, we must confess that the Egyptians at that time used the same letters with the Phenicians.

The opinion most generally received is, that Cadmus, the Phenician, introduced the first Greek alphabet into Bœotia, where he settled B. C. 1500; and this sentiment is supported on the authorities of Herodotus, Diogenes Laertius, Pliny, Plutarch, and others among the ancients,

Greek.

and on those of Scaliger, Salmasius, Vossius, Bochart, and other moderns.

Many believe however, and not without weighty arguments on their side, that the Greeks had an alphabet before the time of Cadmus *. Josephus, on the other hand, in his answer to Apion, about the antiquities of the Jews, says, that the Greeks having failed in producing any authentic memorial of the antiquity of their alphabet, it became afterwards a question, whether the use of their letters was so much as known at the time of the Trojan war, which was decided in the negative.

The original alphabets, as will be shewn, contained only the letters essentially necessary; other single consonants, the double ones, and the long vowels, being the result of subsequent improvement.

The opinion of Montfaucon appears highly probable, that the original alphabet of Cadmus consisted only of the sixteen following letters:

Α Β Γ Δ Ε Ι Κ Λ Μ Ν Ο Π Ρ Σ Τ Υ

together with the extra characters used for numerals, viz. ς or F for 6, and in the Æolic dialect for V or W, and follows E; ϡ after Π for 900; and Ϙ or ϙ for 90, before P; which three characters are evidently from the Phenician alphabet, where they hold the same places.

The honor of adding the other eight is differently assigned by different authors. Montfaucon contents himself with saying, that it seems as probable an opinion as any, that Palamedes, during the Trojan war, added

Θ Ξ Φ Χ

and Simonides, long afterwards, the remaining four, viz.

Ζ Η Ψ Ω

But Westenius, *de linguâ Græcâ*, tells us, that Pythagoras invented the Υ of the original alphabet, as a representation of the path of life.

* See Astle on the origin of writing.

Greek.

Epicharmus, the Sicilian, is also said to have invented the Θ and X, which others give to Palamedes.

I agree with Chishull in considering the H aspirate, as an original radical letter, not only because it is found in all the ancient alphabets, but because there is no other radical from which it could have been derived.

Diodorus Siculus, a writer of great authority, contends that the Pelasgic letters were prior to the Cadmean; hence it is inferred, that the Pelasgic Argive, and the Attic, were of the same origin, and the Cadmean the same with the Æolian and Ionian, which is confirmed by the application of the letters to numbers. This inference, however, appears to be opposed by the general confession, that the Latin, (which we would naturally conclude to have been derived from the Etruscan) is undoubtedly the offspring of the Doric dialect of the Greek. The discussion, however, of this question cannot be expected in a work of this kind.

The alphabets of all languages, as well as the laws of all nations, ought to be in a state of progressive improvement. * It is probable, that the first alphabets were very defective in the number of their characters, and that additions were successively made, when the same letter was observed to represent different sounds.

Greece and Etruria appear to have been the first parts of Europe in which alphabets were used.

The first European alphabet is proved to have been the Pelasgic, or Etruscan, of which the original or radical letters are given in No. 1. and 2.

Astle on the radical letters of the Pelasgians, p. 5. informs us, that "the alphabet, which the *Pelasgi* first brought "into Italy, and which has been called their original al-"phabet, was probably carried out of Phenicia before the "Phenicians themselves had augmented the number of ra-"dical letters, of which it was originally composed. This

* See Astle on the radical letters of the Pelasgi and Etruscans.

Greek 1.

Greek 2.

Greek 3.

a b ĕ f g z h th

i k l m n s p ph

ch r ps t

GREEK.

" alphabet consisted of *thirteen* letters, according to Dr. " Swinton; but according to Father Gori, who appears " to have been better informed, the original alphabet con- " sisted only of *twelve* letters. As these authors differ " materially, it may be proper to give both alphabets."

GREEK 1.

The most ancient inscriptions in the Pelasgian characters and language, are those found at Eugubium, a city in Umbria, in the Apennines, A. D. 1456.

Astle on Writing, p. 64.

This is Dr. Swinton's radical Pelasgian alphabet, and has thirteen characters or sounds.

Astle on the Pelasgian character, p. 5.

GREEK 2.

The radical Pelasgian alphabet of Father Gori, containing twelve characters or sounds, which Astle supposes to be the most correct.

Astle on the Pelasgian character, p. 5.

Astle in the same work, p. 13. thinks the additional letters were derived from the radicals in the following manner, viz.

K diminished, produced the Roman C and Greek Γ.
Π augmented or condensed, became B and aspirated Φ.
Σ becomes Z in most languages.
T naturally produces Δ and Θ.
F or Υ produced O and Ω, and perhaps ȣ.
Ξ is K Σ, and Ψ is Π Σ.
The X was doubtless the guttural sound of Gh or Ch.

GREEK 3.

This Pelasgian alphabet is also taken from the Eugubian tables, and contains twenty letters.

Encyc. Franc. pl. VIII.

Greek 4.

Α	Β	Γ	Δ	Ε	F	Ζ	Η
a	b	g	d	e	f	z	h
Θ	Ι	Ι	Κ	Λ	Μ	Ν	Ξ
th	i	i	k	l	m	n	x
Ο	Γ	Ϡ	Ϙ	Ϙ	Ρ	Σ	Τ
o	p	ss	q	q	r	s	t

Greek 5.

Α Α Α Β Λ Δ ∇ Δ Ε Ε Η Η

a b g d ĕ ē h

Θ Ι Ι Κ Κ Λ Λ Λ Μ Μ Ν Ν

th i k l m n

Ο Γ Γ Ρ Ρ Ρ Ρ Ρ Σ Σ Ζ Σ

ŏ p r s

Σ Τ Τ Υ Υ Φ Χ Ο Ω

t u ph ch ō

GREEK 4.

The alphabet of Cadmus, or the Ionic, B. C. 1500; formed from the Phenician reversed; taken from the coins of Sicily, Bœotia, Attica, &c.

Dr. Barnard's Tables.
Spanheim, p. 82.

GREEK 5.

THIS alphabet (the deficient letters being supplied on the authority of Chishull) is taken from the Sigean inscription *, so called from the promontory and town of Sigeum, near Troy, where it was found. It is engraved on a pillar of beautifully white marble, nine feet high, two feet broad, and eight inches thick; which, as appears by an excavation in the top, and the tenor of the inscription, supported a bust or statue of Phanodicus, whose name it bears; and was undoubtedly erected before the time of Simonides, who flourished 500 years before Christ.

The antiquity of it is evinced by it's being read alternately from left to right, and from right to left; as well as by the state of the Greek alphabet at that time: for we observe, that Simonides had not then introduced the use of the H for the long E, nor the Ω for the long O. Some time after the pillar had been erected, and most probably after the town of Sigeum had come under the power of the Athenians, which happened about 590 years B. C., the first part of the inscription was again engraven near the top of the pillar, with the H and Ω; which, in the original, are supplied by E and O, and where the H is used only as an aspirate, as in modern languages.

Chishull, p. 4.

* Qua nulla in toto Orbe spectabilior, neque genuinæ unquam antiquitatis certioribus indiciis claruit. CHISHULL, p. 3.

Greek 6.

ΦΑΝΟΔΙΚΟ:ΕΙΜΙ:ΤΟΗ
ϽΚΟΦΠΟΤ:ΣΟΤΑΡΚΟΜΡΕ
ΝΕΣΙΟ: ΚΑΛΟ:ΚΡΑΤΕΡΑ
ΝΟΘΕΗ ΙΑΚ:ΝΟΤΑΤΣΙΠΑΚ
ΟΝ:ΕΣΠΡΥΤΑΝΕΙΟΝ:Κ
Υ ΕΛΙΣ:ΑΝΕΜΝΜ:ΑΚΟΔ
ΕΥΣΙ: ΕΑΝΔΕΤΙΠΑΣΧ
ΟΕ ▬ : ΝΕΜΙΑΔΕΛΕΜΟ
ΣΙΛΕΙΕΣ:ΚΑΙΜΕΠΟ
ΙΑΚ:ΣΟΠΟΣΙΑΗ:ΝΕΣΙΕ
ΗΑΔΕΛΦΟΙ

Greek 7.

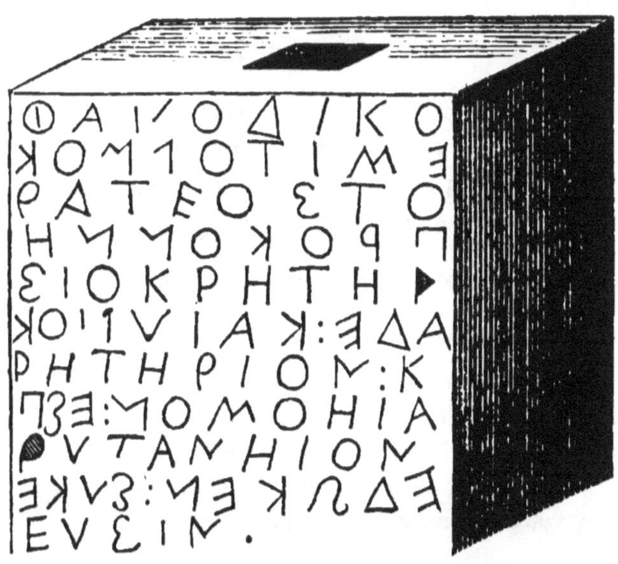

Greek 6.

Is the original inscription; the reading of which, in the common small Greek letter, is here given, observing that every second line of the original is read from right to left; which manner of writing was called βυστροφηδον, as imitating the turn of the oxen at the end of each furrow. This union of the European and Eastern manner of writing in the same piece, was very rarely used after the time of Solon, who probably adopted it, to give his laws an air of antiquity. We cannot imitate this manner of writing, without types cast on purpose, which appears to be unnecessary, as the original is given.

In the common Greek character it runs thus:

Φανοδικο ειμι το Ηερμοκρατος το προκονεσιο: καγο κρατερα καπισταθον και Ηεθμον ες πρυτανειον κδοκα, μνεμα Σιγευευσι. Εαν δε τι πασχο μελεδαινεν εο σιγειες και μ'εποεισεν Ηαισοπος και Ηαδελφοι.

Chishull, p. 4.

Greek 7.

Is that part of the inscription which was copied after Simonides had completed the Greek alphabet, and is as follows, reading every second line from right to left:

Φανοδικο εμι τορμοκρατεος το προκοννησιο κρητηρα δε και υποκρητηριον και ηθμον ες πρυτανηιον εδωκεν συκεευσιν

This secondary inscription varies from the original in one whole word only, viz. υποκρητηριον for επισταθον, which does not alter the sense; and the omission of the words καγω and μνημα; but we observe the regular use of the long vowels, and the omission of the aspirate H.

Greek 8.

Greek 9.

Α	Β	Γ	Δ	Ε	Ϝ	Ζ	Η
a	b	g	d	ĕ	f	z	ē
Θ	Ι	Κ	Λ	Μ	Ν	Ξ	Ο
th	i	k	l	m	n	x	ŏ
Π	Ϙ	Ρ	Σ	Τ	Υ	Φ	Ω
p	q	r	s	t	u	ph	ō

Greek 10.

a		d	e		th	i	k
l	m	n		o	p		
r	s		t	u	chi		

Greek.

The *S* in the original has the two most ancient forms of that letter; in the other, that of the Scythian bow.

We also remark a few errors of the workmen, who cut each of the inscriptions; but the orthography of the last word in No. VII. is either very erroneous, or confirms the opinion that the Greek K had sometimes the force of the Γ or the Latin C.

Chishull, p. 4.

Greek 8.

Contains the real form and magnitude of the letters upon the Sigean marble, viz. the ΕΓΙΣ or SIGE read from right to left in the sixth line of No. 6.

Chishull, p. 4.

Greek 9.

This is the completed Greek alphabet of Simonides, as used on coins and inscriptions in Attica, about B. C. 500. the three last letters are unintentionally omitted.

Dr. Barnard's Tables.
Spanh. Dissert. p. 82.

Greek 10.

The *Nemean*. This alphabet is taken from ancient marbles, on which it is said to have been engraved before the Peloponnesian war, which happened about B. C. 430.

Massey, p. 79.

Greek 11.

Greek 12.

Greek 13.

Greek 11.

The *Delian*. On mount Cynthus, in the isle of Delos, in the Archipelago, are the remains of a stately building; and from inscriptions, (from which this character is taken,) discovered some time since, which mention a vow made to Iris, Serapis, and Anubis, it is conjectured that there stood a temple dedicated to those Egyptian deities, B. C. circa 430.

Encyc. Britan. v. 5. p. 722.
Massey, p. 79.

This alphabet and the preceding furnish us with the origin of the Roman S.——ᶓ Σ Ƨ ƨ S.

Greek 12.

The *Athenian*. Wachteri naturæ, et scripturæ concordia, No. 259, 260, gives this alphabet the same high antiquity as the preceding.

Massey, p. 79.
Duret, p. 670.
Le Clabart, p. 603.

Greek 13.

The *Æolian*. Theseus Ambrosius gives this alphabet as very ancient, and under this name. B. C. circa 400.

Duret, p. 650.
Le Clabart, p. 604.
Fourn. v. 2. p. 217.

Greek 14.

a b g d ĕ z ē th

i k l m n x ŏ p

r s t u ph ch ps ō

Greek 15.

a b g d ĕ z ē th

i k l m n x ŏ p

r s t u ph ch ps ō

Greek 16.

A B Γ Δ E Ι H Θ

a b g d ĕ z ē th

I K Λ M N Ξ O Π

i k l m n x ŏ p

P Σ T Y Φ X Ω

r s t u ph ch ō

Greek 14.

Attick. So called by Fournier, v. 2. p. 217. Le Clabart, p. 491 and 604, says, this alphabet is taken from ancient medals, inscriptions, and bronzes. Duret, p. 670, gives it the title of *Grec Ancien*, about B. C. 400.

Greek 15.

Dorick. Le Clabart, p. 605, and Duret, p. 670, inform us, that this charaĉter was brought from the Levant by curious polygraphists and antiquarians. Fournier, v. 2. p. 217, calls it *Dorick*, B. C. 400.

Greek 16.

Teian. Taken from marbles said to have been of the same antiquity as the Nemean, about B. C. 430.

Massey, p. 79.

Greek 17.

ΟΥΡΙΟΝΕΚΠΡΥΜΝΗΣΤΙΣΟΔΗΓΗΤΗΡΑΚΑΛΕΙΤΩ

ΖΗΝΑΚΑΤΑΠΡΟΤΟΝΩΝΙΣΤΙΟΝΕΚΠΕΤΑΣΑΣ

ΕΙΤΕΠΙΚΥΑΝΕΑΣΔΙΝΑΣΔΡΟΜΟΣΕΝΘΑΠΟΣΕΙΔΩΝ

ΚΑΜΠΥΛΟΝΕΙΛΙΣΣΕΙΚΥΜΑΠΑΡΑΨΑΜΑΘΟΙΣ

ΕΙΤΕΚΑΤΑΙΓΑΙΗΝΠΟΝΤΟΥΠΛΑΚΑΝΟΣΤΟΝΕΡΕΥΝΑΙ

ΝΕΙΣΘΩΤΩΙΔΕΒΑΛΩΝΨΑΙΣΤΑΠΑΡΑΞΟΑΝΩΙ ———

ΩΔΕΤΟΝΕΥΑΝΤΗΤΟΝΑΕΙΘΕΟΝΑΝΤΙΠΑΤΡΟΥΠΑΙΣ

ΣΤΗΣΕΦΙΛΩΝΑΓΑΘΗΣΣΥΜΒΟΛΟΝΕΥΠΛΟΙΗΣ

GREEK 17.

Copy of the inscription upon the base of the statue of Jupiter Urius, the sender of favorable winds, erected at Chalcedon, near the entrance of the Bosphorus, by Philo, the statuary, the son of Antipater, who was patronized by Hephestion, the friend of Alexander the Great.

The following is a correct reading of it in the modern Greek character, with an English translation.

Ουριόν εκ πρυμνης τις όδηγηληρα καλειτω
Ζηνα, κατα τροποιων ιςιον εκπετασας.
Ειτ επι Κυανεας δινας δρομος, ενθα Ποσειδων
Καμπυλον ειλισσει κυμα παρα ψαμαθοις.
Ειτε κατ' Αιγαιην πονλυ πλακα νοςον ερευνα,
Νεισθω, τωδε βαλων ψαιςα παρα ξοανω.
Ωδε τον ευαντηλον αει θεον, Αντιπατρυ παις,
Στησε Φιλων, αγαθης συμβολον ευπλοιης.

See Chishull's corrections at the end of his work. Edit. 1728.

TRANSLATION.

Whoever hence expands his sails, let him
from the stern invoke the protection of
Jupiter Urius.
Whether towards the Euxine he bend his course,
Where Neptune rolls the curling wave among the sands,
Or seek his return towards the Ægean;
To this statue let him offer the votive cake.
In this interesting attitude,
Philo, the son of Antipater,
Represented the benign Deity,
As an omen of a prosperous voyage.

Greek 18.

Α	Β	Γ	Δ	Є	ς	Ζ	Η
a	b	g	d	ĕ	f	z	ē
Θ	Ι	Κ	Λ	Μ	Ν	Ξ	Ο
th	i	k	l	m	n	x	ŏ
Π	Ρ	Σ	Τ	Υ	Φ	Χ	Ψ
p	r	s	t	u	ph	ch	ps

Greek 19.

Α	Β	Γ	Δ	Ε	Ζ	Η	Θ
a	b	g	d	ĕ	z	ē	th
Ι	Κ	Λ	Μ	Ν	Ξ	Ο	Π
i	k	l	m	n	x	ŏ	p
Ρ	Σ	Τ	Υ	Φ	Χ	Ψ	Ω
r	s	t	u	ph	ch	ps	ō

Greek 20.

a	b	g	d	ĕ	z	ē	th
i	k	l	m	n	x	ŏ	p
r	s	t	u	ph	ch	ps	ō

GREEK 18.

This alphabet was in use in the time of Alexander the Great, B. C. 330.

Dr. Barnard's Table.
Spanh. Dissert. p. 82.
Dr. Morton's Table.

GREEK 19.

Taken from the coins of the Antiochi, kings of Syria, three of which name, viz. Antiochus Soter, Antiochus Theos, and Antiochus the Great, reigned from the year 242 to 187, B. C. also on those of the Arsasidæ and other eastern monarchs, as well as some states of Greece.

The French virtuosi call them *Medailles perlées.*

Montf. Pal Gr. p. 143.

GREEK 20.

Of *Virgil.* Supposed to have been invented by this poet, who wrote much on magical subjects, but always in an unknown character.

Fourn. v. 2. p. 222.
Le Clabart, p. 622.

Greek 21.

Greek 22.

Α	Β	Γ	Δ	Ε	ϛ	Ζ	Η
a	b	g	d	ĕ	f	z	ê
Θ	Ι	Κ	Λ	Μ	Ν	Ξ	Ο
th	i	k	l	m	n	x	ŏ
Π	Ϙ	Ρ	Ϲ	Τ	Υ	Φ	Χ
p	q	r	s	t	u	ph	ch

Greek 23.

ΠΕΡΗΜΩΝΟΕΝΤΟΙϹΟΥΝΟΙϹ
ΑΓΙΑϹΘΗΤΩΤΟΟΝΟΜΑϹΟΥ.
ΕΛΘΕΤΩΗΒΑϹΙΛΕΙΑϹΟΥ·ΓΕΝΗ
ΘΗΤΟΤΟΘΗΛΗΜΑϹΟΥΩϹ
ΕΝΟΥΝΩΚΑΙΕΠΙΓΗϹ·ΤΟΝ
ΑΡΤΟΝΗΜΩΝΤΟΝΕΠΙΟΥϹΙΟ
ΔΙΑϹΥΗΜΕΙΝΤΟΙΚΑΘΗΜΕΡΑ
ΚΑΙΑΦΕϹΗΜΙΝΤΑϹΑΜΑΡΤΙΑϹ
ΗΜΩΝ·ΚΑΙΓΑΡΑΥΤΟΙΑΦΙΟΜΕ

GREEK 21.

Of *Apollonius*, a celebrated impostor, and Pythagorean philosopher, a few years before Christ.

Fourn. v. 2. p. 222.
Duret, p. 132.
Le Clabart, p. 690.

GREEK 22.

Of Constantine the Great, A. D. 306.

Drs. Barnard and Morton's Tables.
Spanh. Dissert. p. 82.
Massey, p. 99.

GREEK 23.

A *fac simile* of that ancient and valuable manuscript of the New Testament in the British Museum, presented to King Charles I. in 1628, by Cyrillus Lucaris, patriarch of Alexandria, and is supposed to have been written upwards of 1400 years.

The author was favored with this note a few years ago by the late Dr. Woide.

Greek 24.

ⲁ	Β	Γ	Δ	Є	ς	Ζ	Η
a	b	g	d	ĕ	f	z	ē
Θ	Ι	Κ	λ	Μ	Ν	ξ	Ο
th	i	k	l	m	n	x	ŏ
Π	ϙ	Ρ	C	Τ	Υ	Χ	ω
p	q	r	s	t	u	ch	ō

Greek 25.

ⲁ	Β	Γ	ⲇ	Є	ς	Ζ	Η
a	b	g	d	ĕ	f	z	ē
Θ	Ι	Κ	λ	Μ	Ν	ξ	Ο
th	i	k	l	m	n	x	ŏ
Π	ϙ	Ρ	C	Τ	Υ	Φ	Χ
p	q	r	s	t	u	ph	ch

Greek 26.

α	β	γ	δ	ε	ς	ζ	η
a	b	g	d	ĕ	f	z	ē
θ	ι	κ	λ	μ	ν	ξ	ο
th	i	k	l	m	n	x	ŏ
ϖ	ϙ	ρ	σ	τ	υ	φ	χ
p	q	r	s	t	u	ph	ch

Greek 24.

Of *Justinian the Great*, A. D. 527.
Drs. Barnard and Morton's Tables.
Massey, p. 99.

Greek 25.

Of *Heraclius*, A. D. 610.
Drs. Barnard and Morton's Tables.
Massey, p. 99.

Greek 26.

Of *Leo Isaurus*, A. D. 716.
Drs. Barnard and Morton's Tables.
Massey, p. 99.

Greek 27.

α	ϐ	γ	δ	ε	ϛ	ζ	η
a	b	g	d	ĕ	st	z	ē
θ	ι	κ	λ	μ	ν	ξ	ο
th	i	k	l	m	n	x	ŏ
ϋ	ρ	σ	τ	υ	φ	χ	ω
ü	r	s	t	u	ph	ch	ō

Greek 28.

Α	Β	Γ	Δ	Ε	Ζ	Η	Θ
a	b	g	d	ĕ	z	ē	th
Ι	Κ	Λ	Μ	Ν	Ξ	Ο	Π
i	k	l	m	n	x	ŏ	p
Ρ	Σ	Τ	Υ	Φ	Χ	Ψ	Ω
r	s	t	u	ph	ch	ps	ō

Greek 29.

Α	Β	Γ	Δ	Ε	Ϝ	Ζ	Η
a	b	g	d	ĕ	f	z	ē
Θ	Ι	Κ	Λ	Μ	Ν	Ξ	Ο
th	i	k	l	m	n	x	ŏ
Π	Ϙ	Ρ	Σ	Τ	Υ	Φ	Χ
p	q	r	s	t	u	ph	ch

Greek 27.

This is the earliest specimen of small Greek letters that we have met with, and is found in the Murbac manuscript; in which it is observable, that the ϛ obtains the sixth place, agreeably to the ancient alphabets; and the *iota* has the form of the inverted *eta*, and the *upsilon* follows the *omicron* as well as the *tau*. A. D. 800.

Montf. Pal. Gr. p. 222.

Greek 28.

This alphabet is taken from the Colbertine MS. of the eighth century.

Montf. Pal. Gr. p. 229.

Greek 29.

This character is copied from Massey, p. 99, and was used in the ninth century in the time of Charlemagne.

Drs. Barnard and Morton's Tables.

Greek 30.

Α	Β	Γ	Δ	Ε	Ζ	Η	Θ
a	b	g	d	ĕ	z	ē	th
Ι	Κ	Λ	Μ	Ν	Ξ	Ο	Π
i	k	l	m	n	x	ŏ	p
Ρ	Ϲ	Τ	Υ	Φ	Χ	Ψ	Ω
r	s	t	u	ph	ch	ps	ō

Greek 31.

Α	Β	Γ	Δ	ε	ϛ	ζ	Η
a	b	g	d	ĕ	f	z	ē
ϑ	ι	κ	Λ	Μ	ν	ξ	ο
th	i	k	l	m	n	x	ŏ
ϖ	ϙ	ρ	ϲ	τ	γ	φ	χ
p	q	r	s	t	u	ph	ch

Greek 32.

Ο ταν ακȣσης θυμον και οργην,

μηδεν ανθρωπινον υποπλευσης·

συγκαταβασεως γαρ εστι τα ρ

Greek 30.

This alphabet is taken from a fragment communicated by Anselm Bandurius, supposed to be of the eighth or ninth century.

Montf. Pal Græc. p. 234.

Greek 31.

The Greek of Basil and Constantine, about A. D. 900.

Drs. Barnard and Morton's Tables.
Massey, p. 99.

Greek 32.

This specimen of small Greek letters, joined together in manuscript, is taken from a copy of Chrysostom's homilies on the psalms, in the French King's library; to which I have subjoined the reading in the modern character. This manner of joining the letters in writing was generally used about A. D. 900.

Montf. Pal. Græc. p. 274.

Greek 33.

Αα	Ββϐ	Γγ	Δδ	Εε	Ζζ	Ηη	Θθϑ
a	b	g	d	ĕ	z	ē	th
Ιι	Κκ	Λλ	Μμ	Νν	Ξξ	Οο	Ππϖ
i	k	l	m	n	x	ŏ	p
Ρρϱ	Σϛσς	Ττ	Υυ	Φφ	Χχ	Ψψ	Ωω
r	s	t	u	ph	ch	ps	ō

Greek 34.

Πατερ ἡμων ὁ εν τοις ȣρανοις, ἁγιασθητω το ονομα σȣ. ελθετω ἡ βασιλεια σȣ· γενηθητω το θελημα σȣ, ὡς εν ȣρανω, και επι της γης. τον αρτον ἡμων τον επιȣσιον δος ἡμιν σημερον. και αφες ἡμιν τα οφειληματα ἡμων, ὡς και ἡμεις αφιεμεν τοις οφειλεταις ἡμων. και μη εισενεγκης ἡμας εις πειρασμον, αλλα ρυσαι ἡμας απο τȣ πονηρȣ. ὁτι σȣ εστιν ἡ βασιλεια, και ἡ δυναμις, και ἡ δοξα εις τȣς αιωνας. αμην.

Greek 35.

Απφυς αμων, ο εσσι ενι τα αδιη; αγιασθητω τȣνομα σειο, ελθετω α βασιλεια τευ, γενασθω τ' ȣελδωρ σεοθεν, τως ȣρανοθι, ȣτωσι και γηθι. Τον βεσκερον αμμεων τον επιȣσιον δοθι αμμι τημερον· Και απες αμιν τα οφληματα ημειων, καθα και αμμε, αφιεμες τοισιν οφειλεταισι

Greek 33.

The alphabet of capitals and small letters, as used at the present time; and cast at the Type Street Foundery, where there are eight sizes of the modern character.

Greek 34.

An authentic copy of the Lord's Prayer, from Matthew VI. v. 9, &c. taken from the best editions of the Greek Testament.

Orat. Dom. p. 5.

Greek 35.

This copy of the Lord's Prayer is formed by a combination of various dialects, and differs from classical Greek, nearly as our provincial dialects differ from the stile of our best authors.

Orat. Dom. p. 6.

ημεων. Και μη εισφερησεις αμμας ες ϖειρασμον. Αλλα ρυεο ημεας αϖο τω ϖονηρω. Αμεν.

GREEK 36,

Πατερ ημας, οποιος ισε ενς τως ȣρανȣς. Αγιασθιλο το ονομα σȣ. Να ερτι η βασιλεια σȣ. Το θελιμα σȣ να γινεται ιτζȣ εν τη γη, ως εις τον ȣρανον. Το ψωμι ημας δοσε ημας σιμερον. Και συχορασε ημας τα κριματα ημων, ιτζȣ και εμης σιχορασομεν εκεινȣς, οϖȣ μας αδικȣν. Και μεν ϖλερνης ημας εις το ϖειρασμο. Αλλα σοσον ημας αϖο το κακο. Αμεν.

GREEK 37.

Πατερα μας ο ϖȣ εισαι εις τȣς ȣρανȣς, ας ειναι αγιασμενον το ονομα σȣ; ας ελθη η βασιλεια σȣ, ας γενη το θελημα σȣ, ωσαν γινεται εις τον ȣρανον ετζι και εις την γην. Δος μας σημερον το καθημερινον μας ψωμι. Και σιμπασθησαι μας τα χρεη μας, ωσαν και εμεις συμταθȣμεν εκεινȣς ο ϖου μας, χρεοςȣσι. Και μη μας βαλλεις εις ϖειρασμον. Αλλα ελευθερωσε μας απο τον ϖονηρον. Διατι εδι και σȣ εναι η βασιλεια, και η δυναμις, και η δοξα εις τȣς αιωνας. Αμεν.

Greek 36.

This is the version of Hieronymus Megiserus, in *Specimine quinquaginta linguarum*, A. D. 1603.

Orat. Dom. p. 6.

Greek 37.

This reading of the Lord's Prayer is taken from the manuscript of Dan. Castrosius.

Orat. Dom. p. 7.

Greek 38.

Ω πάτερα μας, ο ϖȣ εισαι εις τȣς ȣρανȣς. Ας αγιαϑη το ονομα σȣ. Ας ελϑη η βασιλεια σȣ. Ας γενη το ϑελημα σȣ, καϑως εις τον ȣρανον, ετζη και εις την γην. Το ψωμι μας το καϑημερινον, δος μας το σημερον. Και συγχωρησε μας τα χρεη μας, καϑως και εμεις συγχωρȣμεν τȣς χρεοφειλητας μας. Και μην μας φερεις εις πειρασμον. Αλλα ελευϑερωσε μας απο τον πονηρον, οτι εδικησȣ ειναι η βασιλεια, και η δυναμις, και η δοξα εις τȣς αιωνας. Αμην.

Greek 39.

Ancient	*Modern*	*English*
εισελϑεν	να εμπη	to enter
κυριος	αφεντης	a lord
νυν	τωρα	now
πορευεσϑαι	να παγη	to go
λευκον	ασπρον	white
ψευδος	ψεμα	a lie
ανϑραξ	καρβȣνο	a coal
ἱππος	αλογο	a horse
αϑροιζεν	να μαζωνη	to assemble
τȣτεςι	ηγȣν	that is
κυων	σκυλι	a dog
οδοντες	δοντια	the teeth

Greek 38.

The Lord's Prayer, taken from the Venice edition of Maximus Gallipolita, which is commonly used in Greece at this time.

Orat. Dom. p. 7.

Greek 39.

A great majority of the words in the modern, are the very same as in the ancient, or classical Greek; in cases where the ancients had two or more words of the same signification, the moderns have sometimes retained only the best, sometimes the worst, and sometimes equal, as αγαπη love, for ancient ερως; αλλος another, for ετερος; αγαπαν to love, for φιλειν; χρονος a year, for ετος; να λεγη to read, for λεγειν, &c. In a considerable number of instances, however, they have introduced new words, and if ever the states of Greece, in the revolutions of empires, should flourish again in population and elegance, it may become a subject of learned speculation to trace their origin.

A few examples are given on the annexed page.

NEW GUINEA.

God	*Wat*	A man	*Sononman*
The devil	*Sytan*	A woman	*Binn*
One	*Oser*	Fish	*Een*
Two	*Serou*	Coco nut	*Sery*
Three	*Kior*	A slave	*Omin*
Four	*Tiak*	Pearls	*Mustiqua*
Five	*Rim*	Beads	*Fin fin*
Six	*Onim*	Iron	*Ukanmom*
Seven	*Tik*	An axe	*Amkan*
Eight	*War*	Gold	*Bulowan*
Nine	*Siou*	Silver	*Plat*
Ten	*Samfoor*	Copper	*Ganetra*
A house	*Rome*	Brass	*Kasnar*
A knife	*Ensy*	Fire	*For*
A musquet	*Piddy*	Water	*War*
A cannon	*Piddybeba*	A dog	*Naf*
The sun	*Rass*	A cat	*Mow*
The moon	*Pyik*	A rat	*Py*

HELVETIAN.

Vatter unser, der du hist in himmlen, geheyligt werd dyn nam; zukumm uns dijn rijch, dyn will geschahe, wie im himmel, also auch uff erden: gib uns hut unser taglich brot: and vergib uns unsere schulden, wie auch wir vergaben unsern schuldneren; and fuhr uns nicht in versuchnyss, sunder erlos uns von dem bosen. Amen.

New Guinea.

This island is also known by the name of Papua.

This specimen of the language of the inhabitants is taken from the vocabulary.

Forrest's Voy. p. 401.

Helvetian.

Swiss. The Lord's Prayer.

Orat. Dom. p. 47.

Hebrew.

Whatever disputes may have arisen among the learned, respecting the antiquity of the Hebrew alphabet, or the manner of writing it, little doubt appears to have been entertained of the antiquity of the language itself. The writings of Moses, and the book of Job, are undoubtedly the most ancient compositions acknowledged in Europe. Both these works exhibit a language arrived at a great degree of perfection, and which must have been in use, as a written, as well as an oral tongue, long before these writings were published, or it would have been useless to have written where none could read.*

Besides a great number of words in the Greek, Arabic, and Celtic, which appear to have been derived from the Hebrew, the very structure of the language points it out as an original one.

The radical words very uniformly consist of two or *three* letters, and the derivatives branch out from them in a manner best calculated to produce precision, and conciseness of expression.

The question, respecting the original Hebrew characters, has undergone abundance of discussion, from the times of the first fathers of the christian church, down to this day. Origen and Jerom, on the authority of the old Rabbis; and among the moderns, Scaliger, Montfaucon, Chishull, and Dr. Sharpe in his treatise on this subject; contend, that the Samaritan was the original Hebrew character, and that the present alphabet was invented after the captivity.

Origen speaks to this effect: In the more accurate copies of the Old Testament, he says, the sacred name of Jehovah is actually written, but in the *ancient* Hebrew let-

* Astle on the origin and progress of writing, p. 12.

ters, and not in those in use at present, which Esdras is said to have introduced after the captivity.

St. Jerom, in his preface to the books of Kings, puts this matter in a still stronger light: he says, the Samaritans often copy the five books of Moses, in the same number of letters as the Jews do, but their letters differ in form, and the use of points; for it is certain, that Esdras, the Scribe, and a teacher of the law, after the taking of Jerusalem, and the restoration of the temple under Zorobabel, invented those other letters which we now use; whereas, before that time, the letters of the Samaritans and Hebrews were the same.

From these passages of Origen and Jerom, we may very certainly conclude, that this was the opinion of the ancient Rabbis and Jewish doctors: but it is very singular, and worthy of notice, that Origen says, that even in his time, the sacred name, in the more accurate copies of the bible used by the Jews themselves, was written in the ancient or Samaritan, not in the Hebrew or modern alphabet, for both Esdras, and the other rulers of the synagogue, who patronized the use of the new characters, believed themselves conscientiously bound to preserve the name of Jehovah in the same letters in which they first received it.

In support of the opposite opinion, the modern Rabbis, the two Buxtorfs, Wasmuth, Schickard, Lightfoot, and P. Allix, (Spanh. p. 69,) &c. contend, that the alphabet now in use among the Jews, is the same that the Law and Old Testament were originally written in from the time of Moses.

Having stated the nature of the dispute, and some of the principal authors on both sides of the question, I think it right to remind my readers, that it is no part of the design of this work to enter minutely into controversies of this kind.

Hebrew 1.

ח	ז	ו	ה	ד	ג	ב	א
hh	z	v	h	d	g	b	a
ע	ס	נ	מ	ל	כ	י	ט
aa	s	n	m	l	k	i	th
	ת	ש	ר	ק	צ	פ	
	t	sch	r	q	tz	p	

Hebrew 2.

hh	z	v	h	d	g	b	a
aa	s	n	m	l	k	i	th
	t	sch	r	q	tz	p	

Hebrew 3.

hh	z	v	h	d	g	b	a
aa	s	n	m	l	k	i	th
	t	sch	r	q	tz	p	

HEBREW 1.

When the ten tribes revolted from Rehoboam, the son of Solomon, they placed themselves under the direction of Jeroboam, the son of Nebat, and settled in Judea, where they preserved their ancient letters; but Esdras, or his son Jesus, who were in the true religion, invented this, from which the present Hebrew is said to be taken.

Duret, p. 129.

HEBREW 2 and 3.

These two alphabets are attributed to King Solomon, by Theseus Ambrosius, in his *Appendice des différentes lettres, et des différentes langues;* but he does not offer any authority. He also asserts, that that prince had many treatises written in them, of which, Apollonius Thianeus was the translator and commentator.

Duret, p. 132

Hebrew 4.

hh z v h d g b a

aa s n m l k i th

t sch r q tz p

Hebrew 5.

hh z v h d g b a

aa s n m l k i th

t sch r q tz p

Hebrew 6.

hh z v h d g b a

aa s n m l k i th

t sch r q tz p

Hebrew 4.

This character was very early used by the Jewish Rabbis in Germany, by whom it was much esteemed, as a handsome current letter, and easy to be written on account of its roundness, wherefore they generally used it in their commentaries and translations.

Duret, p. 132.

Hebrew 5.

This alphabet was used for the same purposes as the preceding, by the Jews of Spain. That both these alphabets were employed for these purposes, is confirmed by Sebastian Munster in his Chaldean grammar.

Duret, p. 132.

Hebrew 6.

This character is taken from an ancient Persian manuscript, but is supposed to be spurious.

Christ. Ravis.

Hebrew 7.

ח	ז	ו	ה	ד	ג	ב	א
hh	z	v	h	d	g	b	a
ע	ס	נ	מ	ל	כ	י	ט
aa	s	n	m	l	k	i	th
	ת	ש	ר	ק	צ	פ	
	t	sch	r	q	tz	p	

Hebrew 8.

אבינו שבשמים: יקדש שמך: תבוא מלכותך: יהי
רצונך כאשר בשמים וכן בארץ: לחמנו דבר יום
ביומו תן לנו היום: וסלח לנו את־ חובותינו כאשר
סלחנו לבעל חובותנו: ואל תביאנו לנסיון: כי־אם
הצילנו מרע: כי לך המלכות וגבורה וכבוד לעולם
עולמים: אמן:

Hebrew 9.

ח	ז	ו	ה	ד	ג	ב	א
hh	z	v	h	d	g	b	a
ע	ס	נ	מ	ל	כ	י	ט
aa	s	n	m	l	k	i	th
	ת	ש	ר	ק	צ	פ	
	t	sch	r	q	tz	p	

Hebrew 7.

The modern Hebrew alphabet. This character was cut at the Type-Street Letter Foundery, under the direction of some very learned Rabbis of the Portuguese synagogue in this city.

Hebrew 8.

The Lord's Prayer, from the Hebrew edition of Munster.

Orat. Dom. p. 9.

Hebrew 9.

The alphabet of Rabbinical Hebrew, of which there are three sizes at the Type-Street Foundery.

Hebrew 10.

בראשית ברא אלהים את השמים ואת הארץ : והארץ היתה תהו ובהו וחשך
על פני תהום ורוח אלהים מרחפת על פני המים : ויאמר אלהים יהי אור ויהי
אור : וירא אלהים את האור כי טוב ויבדל אלהים בין האור ובין החשך : ויקרא
אלהים לאור יום ולחשך קרא לילה ויהי ערב ויהי בקר יום אחד : ויאמר אלהים
יהי רקיע בתוך המים ויהי מבדיל בין מים למים : ויעש אלהים את הרקיע ויבדל
בין המים אשר מתחת לרקיע ובין המים אשר מעל לרקיע ויהי כן : ויקרא

Hebrew 11.

Abhínu schebbaschschamájim; jikkadhésch schemécha; tabhó malchutécha; jehí rezonecha caaschér baschschamajim vechén baárez. lachménu dhebhár jom bejomó then lánu hajjom; uselách lánu eth chobhothénu caaschér saláchnu lebhaalé chobhothénu; veál tebhiénu lenissajón; ki-im hazzilénu merá; ki lecha hamalchúth ughebhurá vechabódh leolám olamím. Amen.

Hungarian.

Mi Atyánc kì vagy az mennyekben, ssenteltessec megâ te neved: jojon elaz te orsságod legyen megâ te akaratod, mint az menyben, ugy itt ez foldonis; az mi mindennappi kenyerünket add meg néküncma; es boczásd meg minéküne az mi vétkeinket, miképpen miis megboczàtunc azoknac, az kic mi ellenünc vetkeztenec: es ne vigy minket azkisertetbe.

Hebrew 10.

This is a specimen of the Rabbinical Hebrew, taken from the beginning of the Pentateuch.

Hebrew 11.

The literal reading of the Lord's Prayer, No. 8.
Orat. Dom. p. 9.

Hungarian.

The Lord's Prayer, from Molnar's Hungarian grammar.
Wilk Ess. p. 435.
Orat. Dom. p. 45.

Hottentot.

One	*Koise*	Bread	*Brè*
Two	*Kamsè*	Butter	*Bingòl*
Three	*Aruse*	Cow	*Gós, Góosa*
Four	*Gna To I*	Cow's milk	*Gósbip*
Five	*Metuka*	Good day	*Dabetè*
Six	*Krubi*	Horse	*Hakva*
Seven	*Gna tigna*	Table	*Heid*
Eight	*Gninka*	Water	*Kamma*
Nine	*Tuminkma*	Mouth	*Kam*
Ten	*Gomatse*	Man	*Kupp*
Father	*Ambup*	Warm	*Sang*
Mother	*Andes*	Knife	*Nórap*
Brother	*Carup*	House	*Omma*
Sister	*Cans*	Eye	*Mu*
Give	*Maré*	Money	*Mari*
Eyes	*Mum*	Breasts	*Samma*
Mare	*Hass*	Cap	*Taba*
Fox	*Giep*	Tiger	*Gvassup*

Huns.

Hottentot.

Taken from the vocabulary of the language.

Thunberg's Travels, Vol. I.

Huns.

This people came out of Scythia into Europe, and in the time of Valentinian, A. D. 376, under Attila, made great ravages in France and Italy; but afterwards at the instance of Pope Leo, settled in Pannonia, which, from the Huns, is now called Hungary.

This alphabet is copied from Fournier, v. 2. p. 209.

New Holland.

A man	*Bamma*	The head	*Wageegee*
A woman	*Mootjel*	The eyes	*Meül*
A father	*Dunjo*	Bones	*Baityebai*
A son	*Tumurre*	Blood	*Garmbe*
Bamboo	*Nampar*	Wood	*Zoocoo*
The sun	*Galan*	Fire	*Maianang*
The clouds	*Wulgar*	Earth	*Poapoa*
A stone	*Walba*	A lance	*Gulka*
A canoe	*Maragau*	To eat	*Boota*
A basket	*Yendoo*	To drink	*Chuchala*
To dance	*Mingooree*	To swim	*Mailelel*
To paddle	*Pelenyo*	Asleep	*Wonananeo*
Sand	*Toowal*	Fish	*Poteea*
Plantains	*Wolbit*	A fly	*Tabugga*
A branch	*Maiye*	The beard	*Waller*
A dog	*Cotta*	The back	*Mocoo*

Jacobite.

New Holland.

Taken from the vocabulary of this language.

Parkinson, p. 148.

Jacobite.

The Jacobites have arranged their alphabet by the Greek, both in name and form, tho' it is much corrupted; they use it chiefly in their holy services; but, for other purposes employ a character between the Armenian and Tartarian; but this is proper to them.

Duret, p. 753.

They are not a nation, but a sect; after one Jacob a heretic, and disciple of a patriarch of Alexandria, attached to the errors of Nestorius.

Fourn. v. 2. p. 277.

Imperial.

Japonese 1.

a	je	i	o	u	fa	fe	fi
fo	fu	ka	ke	ki	ko	ku	ma
me	mi	mo	mu	ssa	sse	ssi	sso
ssu	ja	je	ji	jo	ju	da	de
dsi	do	tzu	ra	re	ri	ro	ru
na	ne	ni	no	nu	n'a	n'e	n'i

IMPERIAL.

This alphabet is a fourth, attributed to Charlemagne, in the beginning of the ninth century, but seems to have been written for some particular purpose.

Fourn. v. 2. p. 272.

JAPONESE 1.

The Japonese have three different alphabets, two of which are in general use among the natives; the other only at court, and among the great.

The specimen we have given is the most common, and, like the Chinese, is written from top to bottom.

Encyc. Franc. pl. XXIV.

JAPONESE 2.

Animal	*Kedamono*	Lion	*Sis*
Arrow	*Ja*	Laughable	*Okaski*
Back	*Senaka*	Man	*Momo*
Breast	*Mone*	Mother	*Fasa*
Carpenter	*Daiku*	Naked	*Hadaka*
Child	*Kodoma*	Nutmeg	*Nikusuk*
Daughter	*Musme*	Oil	*Abura*
Devil	*Oni*	Oysters	*Otjigaki*
Earth	*Tji*	Parents	*Riofin*
Egg	*Tomago*	Pretty	*Migotto*
Face	*Kawo*	Quarrel	*Ijou*
Freeze	*Kogusuru*	Quick	*Faijo*
Girl	*Komusme*	Rainbow	*Nisi*
GOD	*Sin, kami*	River	*Kawa*
Hand	*Te*	Scratch	*Kesuru*
Heaven	*Gokurakv*	Sun	*Fi, nitji*
Interpreter	*Tsusi*	Tongue	*Sta, fita*
Itch	*Kasa*	Town	*Matji*

ICELANDIC 1.

Fader vor thu som ert a himnum, helgest thitt nafn; tilkome thitt riike, verde thinn vilie, so a jordu, sem a himne: gieff thu oss i dag vort daglegt braud; og fiergieff oss vorar skulder, so sem vier fiergiefum vorum skuldinautum; og inleid oss ecke i freistne, heldr frelsa thu oss fra illu; thuiad thitt et riiked, og maatr, og dyrd, in alld er allda. Amen.

JAPONESE 2.

This specimen is taken from a very copious vocabulary of the language.

Thunberg, Vol. 3. p. 1.

In many of the Japonese words I observe the Roman u, when the rest are in *Italic;* as the author is silent respecting them, I presume they have a peculiar sound, for which there is no European accent.

ICELANDIC 1.

The language of this island has been preserved so pure, that even the poorest natives can read, and most of them understand the history of their own country.

Guthrie, p. 454.

The alphabet used by the Icelanders is the Runic, which see.

The specimen annexed is the Lord's Prayer.

Orat. Dom. p. 23.

ICELANDIC 2.

Gret ylgur Ragnvald rytto
Rom-stamir haukar fromast
Kund Lodbrokar; kiendo
Kuillinda valir illra:
Kuóldrido klarar hreldost
Kueid ari már fast reidar
Tijd fiello tar af giodi
Tafnlausir æpto hrafnar.

Thuarr og vid theingils dauda
Thydur morg brád, i hijdi
Skreidast thui bersi skiædur
Skiott marti gráds, of otta:
Ox ódum falu faxa
Frar miog or leiptri tara
Huarma beckur ad hrockin
Hraut gron a baudar nauti.

ILLYRIAN 1.

ICELANDIC 2.

This island having been celebrated for great poets, the annexed stanzas which I have taken from Van Troil's letters on Iceland, p. 215, may be pleasing to some of my readers.

ILLYRIAN 1.

John Baptist Palatin asserts that the Illyrians have two alphabets: the provinces on the eastern side used that which most resembled the Greek, said to have been invented by St. Cyril; those on the west, that of St. Jerom, who is reported to be the author of the annexed; but Aventinus, in the fourth book of his annals, says, that about the time of Christ, a certain person named Methodius, a bishop and native of Illyrium, invented this alphabet; and translated the holy scriptures into it, persuading the people to discontinue the use of the Latin, and the ceremonies of the Roman church. See CROATIAN.

Duret, p. 741.

Illyrian 2.

a b v g d e x z

i k l m n o p r

s t u f h sch ps sci

Indian 1.

hh z v h d g b a

aa s n m l k i th

t sc r q ts p

Indian 2.

a b g d h v z hh

th i k l m n s aa

p tz q r sc t

ILLYRIAN 2.

This alphabet is asserted by Palatin, to have been invented by St. Cyril; it is called Sclavonic, and has much affinity to the Russian.

Duret, p. 738.

INDIAN 1.

Nubian. This is thought to have been the original true character of the Abyssinians, but there is some doubt respecting it.

Duret, p. 383.

Le Clabart, p. 614, says, it was taken from the Grimani library at Venice, and brought to Rome in the time of Sixtus IV. in 1482.

INDIAN 2.

Modern travellers (1619) inform us, that the oriental Indians, the Chinese, Japonese, &c. form their letters upon this model, writing from top to bottom. Jerome Osorius, book 2 of his history of Portugal, says, the Indians use neither paper nor parchment, but mark with a pointed tool upon the leaves of the wild palm, and that they have very ancient books composed in this manner.

Duret, p. 884.

IRISH 1.

b l f s n h d t

c cc m g ng i r a

o u e i

IRISH 2.

b l n t s h d t

c q m g ng sd r a

o u e i

IRISH 3.

b l f s r h d t c

m g ng r a o u e i

ia ai eoi ua eg feo oai oai

IRISH.

General Vallancy, in his essay on the antiquity of this language, has given a full comparative vocabulary of Irish and Punic-Maltese words, with their significations: also a comparative declension of a noun of each tongue, of the same meaning; and he is decidedly of opinion, that it is, through the Pœni or Carthaginians, derived from the Phenician; that, on a collation of this language with the Celtic, Punic, Phenician, and Hebrew, the strongest affinity (nay perfect identity in very many words) will appear; and that it may therefore be deemed a Punic-Celtic compound.

IRISH 1.

This is the most ancient Irish alphabet, and is said to be named *Bobeloth*, from certain masters who assisted in forming the Japhetian language, but it is obviously denominated from Bobel, Loth, it's two first letters.

Ledwich's Antiquities, p. 98.

IRISH 2 and 3.

These two alphabets, called Irish Ogums, the first named *Croabh*, and the other *O'Sullivan*'s, being derivatives from Roman notes, were first stenographic, then steganographic, then magical, and lastly alphabetic. Oga, Ogum, and Ogma are old Celtic words, implying letters written in cypher, and, indirectly, an occult science. Ogan, in Welch, is augury, divination.

Ledwich, p. 90, &c.

Irish 4.

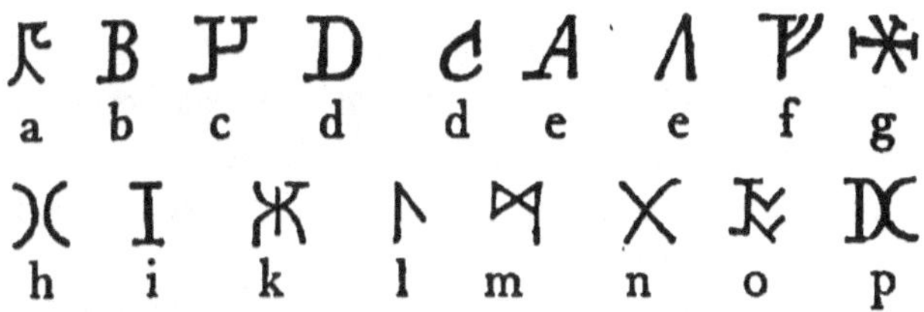

Irish 5.

b l n n f s s h

d t c m m g p r

r a a o u u e i

Irish 6.

Ar nath ata ar neam, Naomtar hainm: Tigead do riogas: Deuntar do toil ar an ttalam, marae do nitear ar neam. Ar naran labtamail tabaird dinn a niu. Agus mait duin ar bfiaca, mar mi maitmidne dar bfeitemnaib fein. Agus na leigt sin a ccatugad, Ar saor in o olc. Oir ir lea fein an riogas, agus an cumas, agus an gloir go siorruige. Amen.

Irish 4.

This alphabet, which is but an imperfect one, is called *Marcomannic Runes;* the latter word being equivalent in sense, and having the same origin as *Ogum.*

Wormius declares, that it agreed with the Runic, both in shape and names.

Ledwich, p. 97.

Irish 5.

This character bears strong marks of a barbarous age, and is, no doubt, the remains of an old magical alphabet; it is called *Bethluisnion na Ogma,* or the alphabet of magical or mysterious letters, the first three of which are Beth, Luis, Nion, whence it is named.

Ledwich, p. 99.

Irish 6.

The Lord's Prayer in the *Bethluisnion* character, " Ex editione Boyleanâ. Lond."

Orat. Dom. p. 57.

This letter was cast at the Letter Foundery in Type Street.

Irish 7.

Ar nathair atá ar neamb, naomhthar hainm: tigeadh do rioghachd, deúntar do thoil ar an ttalâmh, mar do nithear ar neamb; ar narán laéathamhail tabhair dhúinn a niu; agus maith dhúinn ar bhfiacha, mar mhaithm ìdne dar bhféitheamnuibh féin: agus na léig sinn a ca thughadh, achd sáor inn ò olc: oir is leachd

Italian 1.

Padre nostro, che sei ne' cieli, sia santificato il tuo nome; il tuo regno venga; la tua volontà sia fatta, si come in cielo, così anche in terra: dacci hoggi il nostro pane cotidiano; e rimettici i nostri debiti, si come noi anchora gli rimettiamo a' nostri debitori: e non c'indurci in tentatione, ma liberaci dal maligno: perci-

Italian. 2.

Padre nostro, che sei nel cielo, sia sanctificato il tuo nome; il tuo regno venga; la tua volunta sia fatta, sic come in cielo cosi anche in terra: dacci oggi il nostro pane cotidiano: e remittici i nostri debiti, sic come noi ancora rimittiamo á nostri debitori; e non inducici in tentazione; ma liberaci dal maligno; percio che tuo è il regno, e la potenza, e la gloria in sempiterno. Amen.

IRISH 7.

The reading of the Lord's Prayer, from the Biblia Hibernica, Lond. 1690.

Orat. Dom. p. 57.
Vallancey, p, 62.

ITALIAN 1.

The Lord's Prayer; Edit. Genev. 1607.

Wilk. Ess. p. 435.

ITALIAN 2.

The Italian language of the present age is much admired for it's softness, and is spoken by the accomplished in most parts of Europe; it is derived from the ancient Roman or Latin. It would require a volume to trace the changes which gradually converted the old Roman into the language of the present Italians, which is now so polished in point of sound, and rendered so harmonious, as to be thought the best adapted to poetry and music, of any language in the world. The Italian states have different dialects, of which the Tuscan is esteemed the most correct and elegant.

The annexed is the modern reading of the Lord's Prayer.

ITALIC.

ABCDEFGHIJKLM
NOPQRSTUVWXYZ
a b c d e f g h i j k l m n
o p q r ſ s t u v w x y z &

KAMTCHATKA.

GOD	*Kutcha*	The head	*Ktchuin*
The sky	*Keis*	The nose	*Kayakan*
Father	*Inich*	The eye	*Lella*
Mother	*Lachtcha*	The ear	*Illa*
Son	*Pachá*	The mouth	*Chauua*
Daughter	*Schuguiná*	A tongue	*Etchella*
Brother	*Tuiya*	A beard	*Luulla*
Sister	*Milichlch*	Shoulders	*Tuinuinga*
Husband	*Kamjam*	The hand	*Chkatch*
Wife	*Ikitch*	A finger	*Pkotcha*
Boy	*Panaktcha*	The belly	*Haltki*
Man	*Utschkanja*	The back	*Higatch*
A leg	*Htgada*	The flesh	*Tatkhal*

Italic.

The capital and lower-case letters, as now in general use in Europe. This alphabet was called *Venetian*, from it's having been originally cut at Venice; also *Lettres Aldines*, from Aldus Manutius, who invented it about 1512. It is now universally known by the name of *Italic*.

Fourn. v. 2. p. 264.

Kamtchatka.

This specimen of the language is taken from the Vocabularia linguarum totius orbis comparativa, collected by command of the late Empress of Russia. 2 vols. 4to. Petersburg, 1786.

Latin 1.

A B C D E F *G H

I K L M N O P Q

R S T +V +X +Y +Z

Latin 2.

A B G D E F C H

I K L M N O P Q

R S T V X Y Z

Latin 3.

A B C D E F G H

I K L M N O P Q

R S T V X Y Z

LATIN.

The language of the ancient inhabitants of Italy appears to have had the same origin as that of Greece. See ETRUSCAN and GREEK.

It obtained the name of Latin from that part of Italy, formerly called Latium, whence the Romans were ambitious of deducing their descent. As this people devoted themselves almost entirely to wars, for the purpose of extending their empire, and exalting the glory of the Roman name, they paid little attention to the fine arts, 'till they had nearly enslaved the whole world and themselves: this was, doubtless, the reason that they were contented with the Greek alphabet in it's original unimproved state.

Pliny, Book VII. chap. 58, says, " The original Greek " alphabet was nearly the same as the present Latin, as ap- " pears by the Delphic inscription." Tacitus, Book XI. of his annals, says, " the form of the Latin letters is the " same as that of the most ancient Greek."

It is unnecessary to inform the historical reader, that the Romans extended their conquests, and planted a very perceptible portion of their language in every cultivated part of Europe, Asia, and Africa; and that the present Italian, Spanish, Portuguese, and French, are only dialects of it.

LATIN 1.

This appears to be the most ancient Latin alphabet, and is called *Ionic*, the five letters marked * excepted, which have been added since. This character was used about B. C. 714.

Drs. Barnard and Morton's Tables.
Spanheim, p. 114.

LATIN 2.

This alphabet was called *Ionic* and *Attic*, on account of their derivation from the Greeks of these names, and were in use between six and seven hundred years before Christ. It is said to be the foundation of the Roman alphabet now universally adopted.

Fourn. v. 2. p. 268

LATIN 3.

This alphabet was in use at the beginning of the Christian Æra.

Drs. Barnard and Morton's Tables,
Spanheim, p. 114,

LATIN 4.

A B C D E F G H

I K L M N O P Q

R S T V X Y Z

LATIN 5.

A B C D E F G H

I K L M N O P Q

R S T U X Y

LATIN 6.

A B C D E F G H

I K L M N O P Q

R S T U X Y

LATIN 4.

This alphabet appears to have been generally used about A. D. 306.

Drs. Barnard and Morton's Tables.
Spanheim, p. 114.

LATIN 5.

This character, exbibiting a gradual improvement, was employed A. D. 400.

Drs. Barnard and Morton's Tables.
Spanheim, p. 114.

LATIN 6.

We find this alphabet in use about the year A. D. 500.

Drs. Barnard and Morton's Tables.
Spanheim, p. 114.

Latin 7.

a b c d e f ç h

i k l m n o p q

r s t u x

Latin 8.

Λ B 9 D E F V H

I X L M N S O P

Q R Y T

Latin 9.

Pater noster, qui es in cœlis: sanctificetur nomen tuum: adveniat regnum tuum, fiat voluntas tua, sicut in cœlo, et in terra; panem nostrum supersubstantialem da nobis hodie: et dimitte nobis debita nostra, sicut et nos dimittimus debitoribus nostris: et ne nos inducas in tentationem, sed libera nos a malo, quia tuum est regnum, et potentia, et gloria in secula seculorum, Amen.

Latin 7.

This Latin alphabet appears to have been used in the seventh century.

Montf. Pal. Græc. p. 216.

Latin 8.

This alphabet is taken from the Eugubian tables, and is called Arcadian, it being supposed to have been brought from that country by Evander, into Latium.

Encyc. Franc. pl. VIII.

Latin 9.

The Lord's Prayer, from the celebrated vulgate edition of St. Jerom.

Orat. Dom. p. 33.

LATIN 10.

Pater noster qui es in cœlis, sanctificetur nomen tuum; veniat regnum tuum: fiat voluntas tua, quemadmodum in cœlo, sic etiam in terra: panem nostrum quotidianum da nobis hodie: et remitte nobis debita nostra, sicut et nos remittimus debitoribus nostris: et ne inducas nos in tentationem, sed libera nos a malo, quia tuum est regnum, et potentia, et gloria, in secula. Amen.

LATIN 11.

Pater noster, qui es in cœlis, sancte colatur nomen tuum; veniat regnum tuum; fiat voluntas tua, ut in cœlo, sic in terra; et remitte nobis debita nostra, ut et nos remittimus debitoribus nostris: neve nos in tentationem inducito, sed a malo tuere; quoniam tuum est regnum, et potentia, et gloria, in sempiternum Amen.

LATIN 12.

Pater noster, qui es in cœlis, sanctificetur nomen tuum. Adveniat regnum tuum; fiat voluntas tua, ut in cœlo, ita etiam in terrâ. Panem nostrum quotidianum da nobis hodie. Et remitte nobis debita nostra, sicut et nos remittimus debitoribus nostris. Et ne nos inducas in tentationem, sed libera no ab illo improbo quia tuum est regnum, et potentia, et gloria. in secula. Amen.

LATIN 10.

This reading of the Lord's Prayer is copied from the Novum Testamentum Jesu Christi filii Dei, ex Versione Erasmi. Basil. 1570.

LATIN 11.

Copied from Castellio's Biblia Sacra. Frankf. 1697.

LATIN 12.

The Lord's Prayer, taken from Beza's folio edition, Genev. 1598.

LAPLAND.

Isa meidhen, joko oledh tajuahissa; puhettu olkohon siun nimesi: tul kohon siun vvaltakunta; si olkohon siun tahtosi, kvvuin tai vahissa, nyn man'palla, meiden jokapaivven leipa anna mehilen tâna pâivvane, ja anna antexe meiden syndia; kwuin môe annamma vastahan rickoillen: ja âle sata mei tâ kin sauxen

LETTICE.

Musso tæwss kass eeksch dæbbæsim. Swættizlay toop tauwss wardz. Læy eenak mumss tawa kiæmna walstiba, tawss yraatz lay noteek ta wirss sæne mæss kaeeksch dæbbæsim. Musu deenisku maisi dod mumss schoden: un pedod mums mussus paraduss ka mæss peedodam muussim paradneekim. Un næ eewædd

LITHUANIAN.

Tewe musu kursey esi danguy, szweskis wardas tawo; ateyk karaliste tawo, buk wala tawo kayp and dangaus teyp ir andziam es: donos musu wisu dienu dok mumus szedien; ir atlayisk mums musu kaltes kayp ir mes atlaydziam sawiemus kaltiemus: ir newesk musu ing pagundynima; bet giaf bekmus nog pikto. Amen.

LAPLAND.

The Lord's Prayer.

Duret, p. 869.
Wilk. Ess. p. 435.
Orat. Dom. p. 44.

LETTICE.

The Lord's Prayer.

Orat. Dom. Amst. p. 84.

LITHUANIAN.

This is the Lord's Prayer, taken from a bible published in this language. Lond. 1660.

Wilk. Ess, p. 435.
Orat. Dom. p. 43.

LIVONIAN.

Tabes mus, kas tu es eck sckan debbessis: schwe titz tows: waarcz enack mums tows walstibe; tows praatz buska, ksch kan debbes, ta wursan summes: musse denische mayse du th mums schodeen; pammate mums musse grake, ka mess pammart musse parradueken: ne wedde mums louna badeckle: pett passatza mums nu'wusse loune. Amen.

LOMBARD.

LUSATIAN.

Wosch nasch, kensch sy nanebebu, wss weschone bushy me twove: pos hish knam kralestwo twojo: so stany woli tuoja, takhak manebu, tak heu nasemu: klib nasch schidni day nam shensa; a woday nam wyni nashe, ack my wodawamij wini kam naschim: neweshi nass dospitowana: a le wimoshi nas wot slego psheto twojo jo to kralestvo ata moz, ata zest

Livonian.

This is also the Lord's Prayer.

Duret, p. 869,
Orat. Dom. p. 42.

Lombard.

Said to be a Latin alphabet, and to have been used by the Lombards.

Fourn. v. 2. p. 270.
Le Clabart, p. 524.

Lusatian.

The Lord's Prayer.

Wilk. Ess. p. 435.
Orat. Dom. p. 42.

Madagascar 1.

Meaz trangubas tambook trangue vattes tran gue ambone haze, lawa verwan lawa samme samme, trangue France, misse sea lande voolangondre, voolcosse voolangombe mene meinte monguemongue vaque tootolabi.—Oola se meaz moosquine mawoose rez ampaanguinaira oola meaz manne mahaira vinsi ampanguinaira.—Samboorre trangano menewali.—Zaa teaco.—Hanho awyee autanne Madagascar?—Zahai mitondre marmare.—Magnina? Angue, arrey, voora fooshe, sable, firak, lamb, satroo, angamara.—Sos annos anniette.—Zahai rawoo.—Magnina foo annotea? —Zahai tea, engombe, edgondri, enosse, envoosse, accoo, attoole, fuie, vassarre, toolooga, voienguembe, fooshe varre.

Madagascar 2.

Amproy antsica izau hanautangh andanghitsi angharanau hofissahots, vahoüachanau hoaui aminay, fitejannaû hoefaizangh an tane toua andangithsi; mahou mehohanau anrou aniou abinaihane antsica, amahanau manghafaca hanay ota antsica; tonazahai manghafaca hota anreo mauouanay: amanhanau aca mahatetseanay abin fiuetseuetsie ratsi, feha hanau mete zahahanay tabin haratsi an abi. Amin.

MADAGASCAR 1.

Specimen of the language of this island, collected from the *Chansons Madegasses*, by the Chev. de Porny, Paris, 1787. The following is a translation, copied from second volume of the Monthly Magazine, p. 937.

" They will toil to build fine houses of wood and stone, with " great doors and windows, like those of France, decked with " cloths of silk, wool, mohair, ox-hair, red, black, yellow, " green, and all colors."—" The man who toils not is poor, " and hungers, but the man who toils gets drunk, and grows " rich."—" Take the house of my wife."—" I consent to " it."—" Why come you to the land of Madagascar?"—" I " come to bring thee much."—" What is it?"—" Coral, " necklaces, beads, copper, tin, cloth, hats, shoes."—" Thou " art welcome."—" Glad of it."—" What desires thy heart?" — " I want beef, mutton, goats, capons, eggs, fruits, lemons, " oranges, limes, beans, and white rice."

MADAGASCAR 2.

The Lord's Prayer, from Fiacourt's history of Madagascar.

Wilk Ess. p. 435.
Orat. Dom. p. 32.

MAGINDANO.

GOD	*Alatalla*	One	*Isa*
Angel	*Malaycet*	Two	*Daua*
Man	*Tow*	Three	*Tulu*
Woman	*Babye*	Four	*Apat*
Brother	*Pagaly*	Five	*Lima*
Cheek	*Pisni*	Six	*Anom*
Blood	*Lugu*	Seven	*Petoo*
Coach	*Carosse*	Eight	*Walu*
Dance	*Magsaut*	Nine	*Seaow*
Duck	*Pattu*	Ten	*Sanpoolu*
Goose	*Gansa*	Glass	*Chirming*
Gun	*Sanapan*	Hog	*Babuey*
Drum	*Tamboor*	Fish	*Sura, suda*
Hammer	*Dongsu*	House	*Wally*
Heaven	*Langit*	Iron	*Pootow*
Hell	*Inferno*	Kiss	*Pugharo*

MALABARIC 1.

Vanan galil yrûcrà engal pi dàve; unûreya na mam ellatcúm chutamga; unûreya irakiam vara, un manadin paryel à navargal vanatil; cheyuma pelepumylum elarum cheya: andandulla engàl pileycaran carracucù nángal pava carangaley perru: engaley tolxatricù è duvagù ottáde engalucù: polângn varámal vilagù. Amen.

Magindano.

This island, which is one of the Philippines, is called by Lord Anson, in his celebrated voyage, *Mindanao*. The annexed specimen of the language is taken from the vocabulary, in

Forrest's Voy. p. 389.

Malabaric 1.

The literal reading of the Lord's Prayer, from Baldeus's introduction to this language. Amst.

Orat. Dom. p. 27.

MALABARIC 2.

Paramandalang gellile irukkira engel pidawe. Ummudejia namum artschikka padduwadaga. Ummudejia ratschijum wara. Ummudejia sittum paramandalattile scheja padumapole pumijilejum scheja padduwagada. Annannulla engel oppum engellukku innudarum. Engel cadencararukku nangel porukkuma pole nirum engel cadengelei engellukku porum. Engelei tschodineijile piraweschija dejum. Analo tinmeijile ninnu engelei letschittukollum. Adedendal ratschiammum pelamum magimeijum ummakku ennenneikkum undajirukkudu. Amen.

MALABARIC 3.

Unnu undu, rendu rindu, mundu, nalu
1 2 3 4

anji anju, aru, elu, ettu ittu, ombedu,
5 6 7 8 9

pattu, pattinendu, pattirendu, pattimun-
10 11 12 13

du, pattinalu, pattinanju, pattinaru,
14 15 16

pattinelu, pattinettu, pattinombedu,
17 18 19

iruedu, iruedondu, muppedu, natpedu.
20 21 30 40

MALABARIC 2.

Another reading of the Lord's Prayer in the dialect of Tranquebar.

Orat. Dom. Amst. p. 25.

MALABARIC 3.

Taken from the vocabulary of numeration, Thunberg, v. 4. p. 253. but this author seems silent as to the language.

Malabaric 4.

അ	ആ	ഇ	ഈ	ഉ	ഊ	ഋ	ൠ
ă	ā	ĭ	ī	ŭ	ū	rŭ	rū
ഌ	ൡ	എ	ഐ	ഒ	ഔ	അം	അഃ
lŭ	lū	e	ai	o	au	am	ah

ക	ഖ	ഗ	ഘ	ങ	ച	ഛ	ജ	ഝ
k	kk	g	gg	ngh	c	cc	g	gg
ഞ	ട	ഠ	ഡ	ഢ	ണ	ത	ഥ	ദ
gn	t	tt	d	dd	n	t	tt	d
ധ	ന	പ	ഫ	ബ	ഭ	മ	യ	ര
dd	n	p	pp	b	bb	m	j	r
ല	വ	ശ	ഷ	സ	ഹ	ള	ക്ഷ	
l	v	s	ṣz	s	h	l	kc	

Malayan 1.

باڤا كيت يڠ اد د سرڬ

نام مو ديبرسكت

راجت مو منارغ

قندت مو منيد د بوم سقرت د سرك

رت كيت در سهر هر ممبريكن كيت سهر اينل

مك بر امقونل تد كيت دس كيت سقرت

كيت بر امقوناكن سياق برسل كند

كيت

جاغن هنتر كيت كقد چوبهن

MALABARIC 4.

This is the most correct alphabet in use in the Malabar country, whence great care has been taken to obtain it, the first sixteen letters being vowels, and the remaining thirty-five being simple consonants, or radicals.

Propag. Fide, v. 2.

MALAYAN 1.

The Malayan alphabet is the same with the Arabic. The annexed specimen is the Lord's Prayer.

Orat. Dom. p. 20.

Guthrie says this language is thought to be the most pure of any in all the Indies, p. 228.

Malayan 2.

Bappa kita, jang adda de surga, namma mou jadi bersakti, radjat-mu mendarang, kandhatimu menjadi de bumi seperti de surga, roti kita derri sa hari-hari membrikan kita sa hari inila, makka ber-ampunla pada-kita doosa kita, seperti kita berampun-akan siapa ber-sala kapada kita, d'jang-an hentar kita kapada tjobahan, tetapi lepasken kita dari jang d'jakat: karna mu pun'ja radjat, daan kauwassahan, daan berbassaran sampey kakakal, Amin.

Malayan 3.

English	High Malay	Low Malay
The sun	Veiloo	Matt'aree
The moon	Saoo	Boolang
The stars	Nacaistrum	Beentang
The sky	Vanum	Langee
Fire	Tee	Appee
Water	Tanee	Aier
A man	Manizen	Lakee lakee
A woman	Oroopinnoo	Parampooan
Morning	Caluttoo	Pagee
Noon	Ooteha	Taingaree
Evening	Eraoo	Soree
Eyes	Canna	Matta
Ears	Cadoo	Cooping
Cheeks	Caowda	Peepee

MALAYAN 2.

The reading of the Lord's Prayer, copied from the Malay Testament, Edit. Oxf. 1677, in the author's possession.

MALAYAN 3.

A comparison between the High and Low-Malay; the former spoken at Anjenja on the Malabar coast, and called at Batavia the HIGH, or proper; the latter used at Batavia, where it is commonly called the LOW.

Park. Voy. p. 184 and 195.

Malayan 4.

Bapa de somonio, de somonio dunia,
De somonio nigri sujud; [ry Selam;
Dery Christan, dery Cafer, dery Hindoo, de-
Deos, Jehovah, Tuan Alla!

Cassi scio ari iko, makanan, dangang riskimo;
Somonio lain apo apo,
Tuan tow callo by cassi, callo tida,
Tuan alla punio suko.

Adjar scio syang atee, lain oran punio chela,
Adjar scio tutup matto, lain oran punio
Bugimano scio ampong summo lain oran,
Cassi ampong summo scio.

Malayan 5.

باق كامريغ اد د شرگ،
نما مر دسچيكن،
كرجا نمر د دتاغي،
كهند تمر جدياه د بعـمر سغرت دالمر شرگ،
رزق كامر در شهار ه دبريكن اكن كامر
قد هار اين،
دان مغمقن اكن كامر دوش كامر سقرت
كامر مغمقن
اكن بلر غسياق يغ برساله اكن كامر،
دان جاغن ناق كامر قد قرچبان هاث،

MALAYAN 4.

The annexed are three stanzas of Pope's celebrated poem, DEO OPTIMO MAXIMO, or Universal Prayer, in the Malayan tongue, translated by Capt. Forrest.

Forrest's Voy. p. 293.

MALAYAN 5.

The Lord's Prayer in a dialect much differing from that given in No. 1.

Orat. Dom. Amst. p. 19.

Malayan 6.

Bápa kámi jang áda di surga, namà moe diso-etsjíken, karadjäan-moe didatángi, kahendác-moe djadílah di bóemi sepérti dálam surga, ré-ziki kamí déri sahári hári debrikan ákan ka-mi pada hari ini. Daan mengámpon ákan ka-mi dósa kami sepérti kami mengámpon ákan barang siápa jang bérsalah akan kami; daan

Mandarine 1.

Caí tien ngò tem fú chè ngò tem yuén. Ul mîm c'hîm xím. Ul qué lin. Kéi (laî) ùl chì c'hîm hîm yù tí jù yù tien. Yen ngò tèm u-àm ùl kīn jé yu ngò ngò jé yúm leâm. U'l mien ngò chái yù ngò yé xé fú ngò cháj chè. Yeú pú ngò hiù hién yù yeú kan. Naì kieú ngò yù hiūm óo. Qué nêm fő xì ùl yù uû kiúm xí chī xí. yá mén.

Mandarine 2.

Sci gin ta fu ciu zai tien tin. Ngo juon ta fu-min je hhien jam. Ngo juon su gin ciuon sci-eú cui chiai ye. Giu tien gin suō zum ta fun-go juon ta fu foin chungo. Ngo juon ta fú ssi ngo yi cié. Ngo juon ta fú cio ngo ci zui gin gio hai ngo je ciè ci. Ngo juon ta fu jeu ngo guei scien pu mi zui hoh. Ngo juon ta fa chien ngo cu nan. Amin.

Malayan 6.

The literal reading of the preceding Lord's Prayer.
Orat. Dom. Amst. p. 19.

Mandarine 1.

The Lord's Prayer.
Orat. Dom. p. 30.

Mandarine 2.

The Lord's Prayer.
Wilk. Ess. p. 435.

Mangeean.

English	*Mangeean*	*Otaheitean*
A cocoa nut	Eakkaree	Aree
Bread-fruit	Kooroo	Ooroo
A canoe	Ewakka	Evaa
A man	Taata	Taata
A friend	Naoo, mou	
Cloth plant	Taia aoutee	Eoute
Good	Mata	Myty
A club	Pooroohee	
Yes	Aee	Ai
No	Aoure	Aoure
A spear	Heyhey	
A battle	Etamagee	Tamaee
A woman	Waheine	Waheine
A daughter	Maheine	Maheine
The sun	Heetaia matooa	
I	Ou	Wou

Manks.

Ayr ain, t'ayns Niau; Casherick dy rou dt'ennym, Dy jigg dty Reereeaght: Dt'aigney dy rou jeant er y Talloo myr ta ayns Niau. Cur dooin nyn Arran jiu as gagh laa. As leih dooin nyn Loghtyn myr ta shin leih dauesyn ta janoo loghtyn ny noi shin. As ny leeid shin ayns Miolagh. Agh livrey shin veih olk: Son liats y Reereeaght y Phooar as y Ghloyr son dy bragh as dy bragh. Amen.

Mangean.

A comparison between the languages of Mangeea and Otaheite, from the vocabulary.

Cook's Voy. Vol. 1. p. 177.

Manks.

Guthrie, p. 720, says, the language used by the natives is radically Erse, or Irish, with a mixture of Latin, Greek, Welch, and English words; which composition is called *Manks*.

The annexed specimen is the Lord's Prayer.

Bishop Wilson's Works, Vol. 1. p. 460.

MELINDANA.

Aban ladi fissan auari; It cades esmoctacti. Mala cutoca. Tacuna mascitoca coma fissame Chidaleca ghlalandi. Cobzano chefasona agtona fili aume. Agsar lena Cataiano nacfar leman lena galaia. Vualo tadcholnal tagarabe. Lache nagna min ssciratri. Amin.

MENDÆAN.

hh z v h d c b a

aa s n m l k i t

t sh r q tz p

MEXICAN.

Ore rure u bacpe Ereico: Toicoap pavemga tu a va. Ubu jagatou oquoa vae. Charai bàmo derera reco Oreroso leppè wacpe. Toge mognanga dere mi potare vbupè wacpe ige monangiave. Ara ia vion ore remiou zimeeng cori oreve: de guron orevo ore come moa sara supe oregiron javé; Epipotarume aignang orememoauge; Pipea pauem gne ba ememoan ore suy. Emona.

Melindana.

The Lord's Prayer.

Orat. Dom. p. 26.

Mendæan.

The Mendes are a people of Egypt. This alphabet was formed from the Syriac. A. D. 277.

Drs. Barnard and Morton's Tables.

Mexican.

This is the Lord's Prayer.

Orat. Dom. p. 63.
Duret, p. 944.

Mercian.

a b c d e

f g

h i l m n o

p r

s t th u

x y

Mohawk.

Songwaniha ne karongiage tigsideron. Wesagsanadogegtine. Saianaertsera iwe. Tagserre Egniawan karongiagon siniiugt oni ohwonsiage. Niadewigniserage tagkwanadaranondagsik nonwa. Tondagwarigwiiugston ne iungwarigwannerre siniiugtoni siagwadaderigwiiugstani. Neoni togsa dawagsarinet dewadaderageragtonge. Ne sane saedsiadagwags ne kondigserohase. Ikaen saianertsera ne naah, neoni ne kaeshatstenh, neoni ne onwesegtaksera, ne siniahaenwe. Amen.

Mercian.

These alphabets occur on the Anglo-Saxon coins of Eatwald, and Offa and his Queen, of which a plate, with a great variety, is given in Pinkerton's Essay on Medals, Vol. 2. taken from Hickes's Thesaurus.

Mohawk.

The Lord's Prayer.

Orat. Dom. Amst. p. 89.

MOLDAVIAN.

Otze nasi ezie esæ na nebesech: Da sbetætse æme tböe: Da prædet tzarstbie tböe: Da baidet bole tböe iako na nebesech æ na zemlæ; Chliab nasi nasestniæ dazit nam denes: Æ ostabæ nam delggæ nase sakozie æmæ ostablem dailzænikom nasæm: Æ nebaibedæ nasi beæskusevje: Nai æsbabæ nas ot laikabago: Iako tböe est tzarstbo æ sæla æ slaba otzu æ sïnu

MOLQUEEREN.

Oes Veer der iin de hiim'len binne. Jimme nemme word heil'ge. Jimme keuniink-riike kom to. Jimme wolle geschied op d'ierde alliik as iin de hiimmel. Joeoe oes joe oes dageliiks broeoe. En vorjoeoe oes oes schjolden, alliik as wi vorgoeoe oes schjold'ners. Ende en leide oes naat ein vorsiekiinge, mar vorlos oes van de kwoeoe. Want jimmes iis 'et keuniink

MONK'S.

MOLDAVIAN.

The Lord's Prayer, taken from a manuscript in the Bodleian library.

MOLQUEEREN.

The Lord's Prayer.

Orat. Dom, Amst. p. 88.

MONK'S.

The original mode of writing among the ancient Britons, was by cutting letters with a knife upon sticks, either squared or formed into three sides. This is a very ancient alphabet made in that manner, and called *Coelbren y Mynaiç*, or alphabet of the Monks, and was communicated to me by my ingenious friend W. Owen, F. A. S.

NAGARI 1.

अ	आ	इ	ई	उ	ऊ	ऋ	ॠ
a	â	i	î	u	û	ri	rî
ऌ	ॡ	ए	ऐ	ओ	औ	अं	अः
lri	lrî	e	ai	ô	ow	am	ah

क	ख	ग	घ	ङ
ka	kha	ga	gha	nga
च	छ	ज	झ	ञ
cha	chha	ja	jha	nya
ट	ठ	ड	ढ	ण
ta	tha	da	dha	na
त	थ	द	ध	न
ta	tha	da	dha	na
प	फ	ब	भ	म
pa	pha	ba	bha	ma
य	र	ल	व	
ya	ra	la	va	
श	ष	स	ह	क्ष
sa	sha	sa	ha	ksha

NAGARI 2.

Pater noster qui es in cœlis

sanctificetur nomen tuum regnum

tuum adveniat fiat voluntas tua

Nagari 1.

Several of the provinces of India have alphabets distinct from each other, in which they not only write their particular dialects, but even the *Sanskrita*. Indeed most of the alphabets, properly Indian, agree in the number, order, and power of their letters, with this character, which is properly called *Devanâgari*, in which the *Sanskrita* language is most commonly written, and which is the most elegant and approved.

All languages of the *Hindu* class are read from left to right.

Learners are taught to repeat the *Devanâgari* alphabet according to the annexed very admirable arrangement, which was obligingly communicated to me by my learned friend Charles Wilkins, Esq. F. R. S.

Read *a*, *â*; *i*, *î*; *u*, *û*; &c. *ka*, *kha*; *ga*, *gha*; &c.

Nagari 2.

The Pater Noster in this character, taken from the Encyc. Franc. pl. 17.

NORMAN 1.

NORMAN 2.

ANGLO NORMAN.

Norman 1.

The Normans, Northmans, or people from the north, emigrated from Denmark, Sweden, Norway, &c. and spread themselves over Gaul, but particularly Neustria, which name they soon changed to Normandy ; and during the ravages they were making upon the coast, and other parts, before they could settle themselves, to cover their deliberations and councils, they invented a new alphabet, (according to Bede) in which were only ten principal characters, much like Greek; the other fourteen were formed by uniting those to others, as in the annexed specimen.

Duret, p. 866.

Norman 2.

This alphabet is also given on the authority of the venerable Bede.

Duret, p. 866.

Anglo-Norman.

Called by Astle modern Gothic; by the French *Lettres Tourneures;* they were much used in adorning and illuminating Roman missals, from one of which the annexed specimen was taken.

Nootka Sound.

A man	*Tanass*	A canoe	*Shapats*
The sun	*Opulszthl*	A song	*Oonook*
The moon	*Opulszthl*	A paddle	*Oowhabbe*
A mount	*Noohchai*	Fire	*Eeneek*
A house	*Mahtai*	Yes	*Ai, aio*
Water	*Chauk*	No	*Wook, wik*
Food	*Haoome*	The wind	*Okumha*
A bow	*Moostatte*	A comb	*Suchkas*
An arrow	*Tseehatte*	The hair	*Apsoop*
To kill	*Seehsheetl*	The head	*Oooomitz*
The teeth	*Cheecheets*	The eye	*Kussee*
The nose	*Neets*	The ear	*Papai*
The cheek	*Aamiss*	The chin	*Eehthlux*
The beard	*Apuxim*	The face	*Eslulszth*
The lips	*Eethluxoot*	The arm	*Aapso*
The nipple	*Eneema*	The nails	*Chushchuh*
A porpoise	*Aiahtoop*	A knot	*Mitzsleo*
A bracelet	*Klaklasm*	Give me	*Kaatl*

Norwegian.

Wor fader du som est y himmelen, gehailiget worde dit nafn; tilkomma os riga dit, din wilia geskia paa jorden, som handt er udi himmelen: giff os y tag wort dagliga brouta; och forlaet os wort skioldt, som wy forlata wora skioldonar: och lad os icke komma voi fristelse, man frals os fra onet; thy rigit er dit, macht, och kracht fra evighait til evighait.

NOOTKA SOUND.

Taken from the vocabulary of this language, collected and formed by the late Capt. Cook.

Cook's Voy. v. 3. p. 542.

NORWEGIAN.

The Lord's Prayer.

Orat. Dom. p. 48.

Norton Sound.

Hair	*Nooit*	Eye-brows	*Kameluk*
Eyes	*Enga*	Nose	*Ngha*
Cheek	*Oollooak*	Ear	*Shudeka*
Lips	*Hashlaw*	Beard	*Oongai*
Chin	*Ganluk*	Arm	*Dallek*
Hand	*Aishet*	Nails	*Shetooe*
Thigh	*Kokdoshac*	Leg	*Kanaiak*
Foot	*Etscheak*	Sun	*Maje*
Sea	*Emai*	Water	*Mooe*
Canoe	*Caiac*	Paddle	*Pangehon*
Iron	*Shawik*	No	*Ena*
Yes	*Eh*	One	*Adowjak*
Two	*Aiba*	Three	*Pingashook*
Four	*Shetamik*	Five	*Dallamik*

Nova Zembla.

Otcse naz icse ti nanabezi, Pozuetytze ime tye, Pridi czarztvo tye, Budi uola tya kako unebezi tako nazemli, Hlyb naz zakdan dynam danacz, J odpuzi nam duge naze kako imi odpuzymo doznikam nazim, Jnauedi naz unapazet, Da izctaui naz od zla. Amen.

Norton Sound.

Taken from the table, to shew the affinity between the languages spoken at Oonalashka and Norton Sound, and those of the Greenlanders and Esquimaux.

Cook's Voy. v. 3. p. 554.

Nova Zembla.

The Lord's Prayer.

Orat. Dom. Amst. p. 80*.

Otaheite.

Father	*Mituatane*	Mother	*Mituaheine*
The skin	*Ewey*	Blood	*Matee*
The veins	*Ewaowa*	The hair	*Eraowroo*
The lips	*Eooto*	The teeth	*Eneeho*
A rat	*Eyoare*	A bird	*Manoo*
A seal	*Ehoomè*	A louse	*Oatoo*
Sea-weed	*E reemo*	Bread-fruit	*Ooroo*
Wood	*Etoomoo*	A stone	*Owhai*
Fire	*Wahaa*	Light	*Eahei*
Water	*Avy*	Wind	*Matai*
Clouds	*Eata*	Smoke	*Eohoo*
The sun	*Manaha*	The moon	*Marama*
A ship	*Paee*	A bonnet	*Aihoo*

Oonalashka.

The hair	*Emelach*	Eye brow	*Kamlik*
The eye	*Dhac*	The nose	*Anosche*
The cheek	*Oolooeik*	The lip	*Adhee*
The teeth	*Agaloo*	The chin	*Ismaloch*
The neck	*Ooioc*	The breast	*Shimsen*
A finger	*Atooch*	The nails	*Cagelch*
A thigh	*Cachemac*	A leg	*Ketac*
The foot	*Ooleac*	The sun	*Agadac*
The sky	*Enanac*	A cloud	*Aiengich*
The wind	*Caitchee*	The sea	*Alaooch*
Fire	*Keiganach*	Wood	*Hearach*
A knife	*Kamelac*	A house	*Oolac*

OTAHEITE.

Taken from the vocabulary of the language.

Park. Voy. p. 51.

OONALASHKA.

This specimen is taken from the table of affinity between the languages spoken at OONALASHKA and NORTON SOUND, and those of the GREENLANDERS and ESQUIMAUX.

Cook's Voy. vol. 3. p. 554.

ORCADIAN.

Favor i iri chimrie, helleur ir i nam thite, gilla cosdum thite cumma, veya thine mota vara gort o yurn sinna gort i chimrie, ga vus da on dalight brow vora, firgive vus sinna vora sin vee firgive sindara mutha vus, lyv us & ye i tuntation, min delivera vus fro olt ilt. Amen.

PALMYRAN.

hh z v h d g b a

aa s n m l k i th

t sh r q ts p

POLISH.

Oicze náss, ktorys jest w niebiesiech. Swiecsie imic twoie. Przydz krolestvo twoie. Badz wola twa, jako wniebie, táky ná ziemi. Chlebá nass ego powessedniego day nam dzisia. Y od pusc nam nasze winy, ja koymy od pusec zamo nássym winowajcom. Ynie w wodz nas na pokusseme. Ale nas zbaw ode zkego. Abowiem twoje jest krolestwo, y moc, y chwata, na wieki. Amen.

Orcadian.

The Lord's Prayer.

Orat. Dom. p. 65.

Palmyran.

This alphabet, which has great affinity to the Hebrew, and is written from right to left, was first decyphered by the late celebrated Abbé Barthelemi.

Encyc. Franc. pl. V.

Polish.

The Lord's Prayer, from a bible in this language, Dantz. 1632.

Wilk. Ess. p. 435.
Orat. Dom. p. 58.

PELEW ISLANDS.

A man	*Arracat*	A woman	*Artheil*
A child	*Nalakell*	A chief	*Rupack*
A father	*Cattam*	A mother	*Catheil*
A wife	*Morwakell*	A boy	*Talacoy*
A friend	*Sucalie*	The head	*Botheluth*
The teeth	*Ungelell*	The arms	*Kimath*
The body	*Kalakalat*	The blood	*Arrassack*
Bones	*Oroosock*	A spoon	*Trir*
A knife	*Oyless*	A cup	*Pewell*
A bason	*Quall*	Yams	*Cocow*
Plantains	*Too*	A torch	*Outh*
Fire	*Karr*	A town	*Morabalon*
Smoke	*Katt*	A rat	*Pyaap*

PERSIAN 1.

kheh	feh	reh	teh	scheh	deh	ouéh	ueh
meh	schieh	leh	hemeh	żeh	deh	yeh	kha
queh	ah	i	hoüeh	i	teheh	oun	en
deh	ho	teh	enkeh	sch	kieh	hheh	gheh
gieh	dgeh	neh	hayeh	gniéh	pa	seh	eh

Pelew Islands.

This vocabulary of the language is taken from

Guthrie, p. 164.

Persian 1.

This is the alphabet of the *Gaures*, or ancient Persians, who were worshipers of fire.

Encyc. Franc. pl. XV.

PERSIAN 2.

اي پدر ما که در آسمان
پاک باشد نام تو
بيايد پادشاهي تو
شود خواست تو همچنانکه در آسمان نيز
در زمين
بده مارا امروز نان کفاف روز مارا
ودرگذار مارا گناهان ما چنانکه ما نيز
ميگذاريم عرمان مارا
ودر آزمايش مينداز مارا
ليکن خلاص کن مارا از شرير

PERSIAN 3.

Ei padere ma kih der osmon. Pak basched nâm tou. Beyayed padschahi tou. Schwad chwáste tou hemzjunánkih der osmon nîz der zemîn. Bideh mara jmrouz nân kefaf rouz mara. Wuḍargudshar mara konahan ma zjunankih ma niz migudhsarim ormân mara. Wudar ozmajisch minedaz mara. Likin chalasd kun mara ez scherire. Beraj ankih melcut wunirumendi w'a-tsemet ez on toust vuta ebed ebedi 'lebedi. Amin.

Persian 2.

The Lord's Prayer, from Wheloc's four Evangelists in this character.

Orat. Dom. p. 17.

Persian 3.

The literal reading of the above.

Wilk Ess. p. 435.
Orat. Dom. p. 17.

Persian 4.

Ei padere ma kih der osmoni. Pak basched nâm tu. Beyayed padschahi tu. Schwad chwáste tu hemzjunánkih der osmon nîz der zemîn. Bdéh mára jmrouz nân kefáf rouz mara. Wadargudsar mara konáhan ma zjunankih ma niz migsarim ormân mara. Wodar ozmajisch minedâz mara. Likin chalás kun mara ez scherir. Beraj ankih melcut wanirumendi w'a-semet ez on tust ecnoun wota ebed ebed 'i lebedi. Amin.

Persian 5.

Namoz Hasrath Issa. Ei peder moh ki der aosmoni. Nahm ssetthuda kiarda sheued padeschahi tu biagad. Araadeh tu bedgia awerdah sheved derssamin ki dziun der osmon. — Nam hererouss imerouss bæmo bærsan. Ve giunoh moh meof kiunid csenancsi moh. Uschanera ki bemoh giunoh kerda end aafu fermaüm ve derweswesse. Sheittan mahrah mefkiun amma essu mahrah chellos kiunid ki paddeschai tu. Ve dgelalettu ve kuddret tu giawid baschad. Amin.

PERSIAN 4.

The literal reading of the Lord's Prayer in the vulgar dialect.

Orat. Dom. Amst. p. 9.

PERSIAN 5.

The Lord's Prayer in the Jaghuthian dialect.

Orat. Dom. Amst. p. 10.

Persian 6.

دلا گر روشنی شمع برافروز
ز شمع آتش پرستیدن بیاموز
ز خاطر دور کن آتش پرستی
در آتش خانه خاطر نشستی

Persian 7.

tcha	gjia	gha	pa	ba	ă	â	â
tha	cha	zha	za	ou	va	ha	da
sa	na	ma	ta	gha	ca	i	ya

Poconchi.

Catat taxah vilcat; nimta incaharçihi avi; inchalita avihauripan cana. Invanivita nava yahvir vacacal, he in vantaxah. Chaye runa cahuhunta quih viic. Naçachtamac, he incaçachve quimac ximacquivi chiqvih. Macoacana chipam catacchyhi; coaveçata china unche tsiri, mani quiro, he inpui. Amen.

Persian 6.

A verse taken from an ancient Persian manuscript in the possession of Major Ouseley.

Persian 7.

This alphabet, which is taken from Hyde's edition *de Religione veterum Persarum*, is called Zend or Pazend, and is supposed to have been used by Zoroastre.

Encyc. Franc. pl. 16.

Poconchi.

The Lord's Prayer.

Wilk. Ess. p. 435.
Orat. Dom. p. 63.

PHENICIAN 1.

a b c d e f g h

i k l m n o p q

r s t v x y z z

PHENICIAN 2.

hh z v h d g b a

aa s n m l k s th

t sch r q ts p

PHENICIAN 3.

k i hh v h d b a

r q ts aa s n m l

t sh

Phenician.

Chronologers and historians (see Jackson's Chronological Antiquities, Vol. III.) render it sufficiently probable, that the Phenicians had alphabetical characters as early as any people in the world: and tho' no writings in that language have descended to our time, we are, by no means, destitute of sufficient authority for the number and form of their letters. The ancient Greeks called the Phenicians Pelasgi *quasi* Pelagii, or wanderers, from *Pelagus*, the sea; and, as we have already observed, the Pelasgian Greeks, as well as the Thebans and Italians, undoubtedly received their letters from the Phenicians.

It is beyond the limits of this work to give authorities for every individual letter, but I trust my readers will be satisfied with those subjoined.

Phenician 1.

This character has been falsely called Syriac, but it is more properly Phenician, or Ionic, being written from left to right, and having nothing in it's form in common with those letters which compose the Syriac alphabets.

Duret, p. 366.

Phenician 2.

This character, which is attributed to Scaliger, is given by Spanheim, p. 80, also in Montf. Pal. Græc. p. 122.

Phenician 3.

This alphabet is handed to us on the authority of the late Abbé Barthelemy, who is said to have taken it from inscriptions preserved in Malta, and from Syrian medals.

Encyc. Franc. pl. V.

PHENICIAN 4.

n m hh h h d b a

t sh r q aa

PHENICIAN 5.

hh z v h d g b a

ts aa s n m l k i

t sh r

PHENICIAN 6.

i hh v h d g b a

sh r q aa n m l k

t

PHENICIAN 4.

This character, which is also given on the same authority as the preceding, is taken from Sicilian coins.

Encyc. Franc. pl. V.

PHENICIAN 5.

This Phenician alphabet is taken from inscriptions preserved in cyphers, and is mentioned by Pocock.

Encyc. Franc. pl. V.

PHENICIAN 6.

This alphabet, which is given on the authority of the three preceding, is taken from an inscription lately discovered in Malta.

Encyc. Franc. pl. V.

Phenician 7.

a

b

g

d

e

v

ch

i

c

l

m

n

o

z

k

r

s

t

PHENICIAN 7.

Great doubts being entertained of the correctness of the preceding Phenician characters, particularly the two first, I have been favored by my learned friend and antiquary, the Rev. S. Henley, with the annexed alphabetic arrangement, verified from coins and inscriptions by himself, except the ( ) for *oins*, and the same for *pe*, which were adopted on the authorities of Dutens and Bayer.

One	*Keirrk*
Two	*Theirh*
Three	*Neisk*
Four	*Taakhoun*
Five	*Keitschine*
Six	*Kleitouchou*
Seven	*Takatouchou*
Eight	*Netskatouchou*
Nine	*Kouehok*
Ten	*Tchinecate*
Eleven	*Keïrkrha-keirrk*
Twenty	*Theirha*
Thirty	*Neiskrha*
Forty	*Taakhounrha*
Fifty	*Keitschinerha*
Sixty	*Kleitouchourha*
Seventy	*Tatatouchourha*
Eighty	*Netskatouchourha*
Ninety	*Kouehokrha*
A hundred	*Tchinecaterha*

Port des Francais.

Vocabulary of numeration of Port des Francais.
Pérouse, Vol. 2. p. 152.

Philosophic 1.

Our father who art in heaven, thy name be hallowed, thy kingdom come, thy will be done so in earth, as in heaven, give to us on this day our bread expedient, and forgive us our trespasses, as we forgive them who trespass against us, and lead us not into temptation but deliver us from evil, for the kingdom and the power, and the glory is thine, for ever and ever. Amen. So be it.

PHILOSOPHIC I.

The annexed is an attempt of the late learned Bishop Wilkins towards a real character, and philosophical language; but he expresses himself sensible, that this contrivance is not brought to that degree of perfection to which it might have been upon further consideration and practice. For the information of my curious readers, I refer him to

Wilk. Ess. p. 421.

Philosophic 2.

Hαι coba ȣȣ ιa ril dad, ha bαbι ιo sȣymtα, ha salba ιo velcα, ha tαlbi ιo vemgȣ, mȣ ril dady me rιl dad ιo velpι rαl αi ril ι poto hαι sαba vaty, na ιo sȣeldiȣs lαl αι hαι bαlgas me αι ιa sȣeldyȣs lαl eι ȣȣ ια vαlgas rȣ αι, na mι ιo velco aι, rαl bedodlȣ nil ιo cȣalbo αι lal vαgasιe, nor αl salba, na αl tado, na αl tadalα ιo ha piȣbyȣ mȣ ιo. Amen.

Philosophic 3.

Yȣr fádher hȣitsh art in héven: Hαlloed bi dhyi nαm. Dhyi cingdym cym. Dhyi ȣil bi dyn in erth az it is in héven. Giv ys dhis daι yȣr daιlι bred: and fαrgiv ys yȣr trespassez, az ȣι fαrgìv dhem dhat trespass against ys. And léd ys nαt intȣ temptasiαn, byt deliver ys frαm ivil. Amen.

Philosophic 4.

o	*α*	*a*	*e*	*i*	*u*	*y*	*h*
ō	aw	ā	ĕ	ēē	oo	u	huh

g	*k*	*ſh*	*ŋ*	*n*	*r*	*t*	*d*	*l*
gi	ki	sh	ng	n	r	t	d	l

ſ	*z*	*ħ*	*ħ*	*f*	*v*	*b*	*p*	*m*
s	ez	th	dh	f	ev	b	p	m

Philosophic 2.

Another curious attempt of Dr. Wilkins, which he has fully explained in his essays, p. 421, &c.

Philosophic 3.

This is also another example of the Doctor's ingenuity, for which see his essays, p. 435.

Philosophic 4.

In a very curious letter from the late Dr. Franklin, in answer to Miss S****, written in this character, according to the usual mode of spelling and pronunciation, the reader will find the Doctor's arguments for, and recommendation of, his reformed mode of spelling. See Dr. F's. Political, Miscellaneous, and Political Pieces, 8vo. Lond. 1779. p. 473.

The alphabet is copied in the order and manner given by the author, p. 470.

Portuguese 1.

Padre nosso, questas nos ceos, sanctificado seia otu nome; venha à nos o teu reino, sea feita à tua voluntade, assi nos ceos, come na terra. Opao nosson de cadadia, da nolo oie nestro dia, e perdoa a nos sennor as nossas dividas, assi como nos perdoamos aos nossos dividores e naon nos dexes cahir in tentacaon, mas libra nos do mal. Amen.

Portuguese 2.

Pae nosso que estás n'os ceos, sanctificado sega o teu nome, venna o teu reyno, seja feita a tua vontade assi n'a terra como n'o ceo; O paõ nosso de cadadia nos dá hoje, e perdoa-nos nossas dividas, assi como nos perdoamos nossos devedores; e naõ nos metas emtas tentaçaõ, mas livra nos de mal. Porque teu he o

Portuguese 3.

Nosso pay que estás n'o c'eo, santificado seia teu nome, venha teu reyno, tua vontade se faça na terra, como n'o ceo; dà nos oje nosso paõ quotidiano, et perdoanos nossos trespassos assi como nos perdoamos a os que trespassaõ contra nos; et naõ nos tragas à tentaçaõ, mas livra nos do mal: porque teu he o reyno,

PORTUGUESE.

This language does not differ materially from that of Spain, but the pronunciation is harsher.

It is spoken on all the coasts of Africa and Asia, as far as China, but mixed with the languages of the several nations in those distant regions.

Guthrie, p. 813.

PORTUGUESE 1.

The Lord's Prayer, as used about 200 years ago.

Wilk. Ess. p. 435.
Orat. Dom. p. 38.

PORTUGUESE 2 and 3.

These two readings of the Lord's Prayer are given in David Wilkins's edition of Chamberlayne's Orat. Dom. p. 46.

Portuguese 4.

Padre nosso que estais nos çêos, santificado seja o vosso nome, venha a nôs o vosso reyno: seja feita a vossa vontade assim na terra, como no çeo, o pão nosso de cada dia nos dai hoje; perdoai as nossas devidas assim como nos perdoamos a os nossos devidores, e não nos deixeis cahir em tentação, mas livrai-nos de tudo o mal. Amen.

Prince William's Sound.

Akashou	*What's the name of it*
Namuk	*An ear ornament*
Lukluk	*A brown shaggy skin*
Aa	*Yes*
Natooneshuk	*The sea-otter's skin*
Keeta	*Give me something*
Naema	*Exchange with me*
Ooonaka	*Belonging to me*
Ahleu	*A spear*
Weena Veena	*Stranger!*
Keelashuk	*Guts*
Tawuk	*Keep it*
Whaehai	*Shall I keep it?*

Chilke	*One*	Koeheene	*Five*
Taiha	*Two*	Takulai	*Six*
Tokke	*Three*	Keichilho	*Seven*
Chukelo	*Four*	Kliew	*Eight*

Portuguese 4.

The Lord's Prayer in the modern tongue, with which I was favoured by a gentleman well acquainted with the language.

Prince William's Sound.

A specimen taken from a vocabulary of the language in Cook's last voyage, Vol. 2. p. 375.

PRUSSIAN 1.

Thawe nuson kas thu asse andangon, swintin wirst tais Emmens, pergeis twais laeims, twais quaits audasseisin nasemmey key andangon, nusan deininan geïttin dais numons schindeinan, bha attwerpeis noumans nuson anschautins, kay mas atwerpimay nuson anschautnikamans, bhany wedais mans enperbandan, sclait is rankeis mans assa wargan. Amen.

PRUSSIAN 2.

Thawe nouson kas thou æsse endengon. Swytits wirse twais emmens. Parey sey noumans twayia ryeky. Tways quaits audaseysin na semiey kay endengon. Nouson deyninan geytiey days noumans schindeynan. Bhæ etwerpeis noumans nouson anschautins, kay mes etwerpymay nouson anschautinekamans. Emmen.

PRUSSIAN 3.

Nossen thewes cur tu es delbes. Sehwiz gesger thowes wardes. Penag mynys thowe mystlalstibe. Toppes pratres gircad delbeszisne tade tymnes sennes worsinny. Dodi nomimes an nosse igdenas magse. Unde geitkas pamas numas musse nozegun cademas pametam nusson pyrtainekans. No wede numus padam padomam, swalbadi mumes newuse. Jesus Amen.

Prussian 1.

The Lord's Prayer, from Chr. Hartknoch.

Orat. Dom. Amst. p. 85.

Prussian 2.

This reading of the Lord's Prayer is also given on the authority of the same author.

Orat. Dom. Amst. p. 86.

Prussian 3.

The Lord's Prayer, on the authority of Simon Gronovius.

Orat. Dom. Amst. p. 86.

ROMAN.

ABCDEFGHIJKLM
NOPQRSTUWXYZ
abcdefghijklmn
opqrſstuvwxyz&

RUNIC 1.

a b c d e f g h

i k l m n o p q

r s t v x y z

RUNIC 2.

Fader uor som est i himlum, halgad warde thitt nama. Tilkomme thitt rikie. Skie thin vilie, so som i himmalan, so och po jordanne. Wort dachlicha brodh gif os i dagh. Ogh forlat os uora skuldar, so som ogh vi forlate the as skyldighe are. Ogh inled os ikkie i frestolsan, utan frels os ifra ondo. Ty rikiad ar thitt ogh maghtan, ogh harligheten. Amen.

Roman.

The capital alphabet which is now generally adopted and used throughout Europe, is said to have been derived from the Attic and Ionic Greek and Latin, the latter of which is given in No. 2. page 172 of this work. The lower case, or small letters, seem to have been formed from other Latins, Lombard, and Saxon characters.

The annexed alphabets are the Two-Line English of the Type-Street Foundery.

Runic 1.

Several nations of the North used this character, which is derived from the Mæso-Gothic. The annexed alphabet is copied from

Encyc. Franc. pl. X.

Runic 2.

The reading of the Lord's Prayer.

Orat. Dom. p. 22.

Russian 1.

Аа	Бб	Вв	Гг	Дд	Ее	Жж	Ss
a	b	v	g	d	e	j	z
Зз	Ии	Іï	Кк	Лл	Мм	Нн	Оо
z	i	ï	k	l	m	n	o
Пп	Рр	Сс	Тт	Уу	Фф	Хх	Цц
p	r	s	t	u	ph	ch	tz
Чч	Шш	Щщ	Ъъ	Ыы	Ьь	Ѣѣ	Ээ
ch	sch	schtsch	yerr	yerì	yer	yat	é
Юю	Яя	Ѳѳ	Ѵѵ				
yu	ya	th	ischitza				

Russian 2.

Отче нашъ, иже еси на небесѣхъ, да святится имя твое, да пріидетъ царствіе твое, да будетъ воля твоя, яко на небеси и на земли. Хлѣбъ нашъ насущныи даждъ намъ днесъ. И остави намъ долги наша, якоже и мы оставляемъ должникомъ нашимъ. И ни введи насъ во искушеніе, но избави отъ лукаваго. Яко твое естъ царство и

RUSSIAN 1.

The annexed characters were cut at the Letter-Foundery in Type-Street, from alphabets in the *Vocabularia totius orbis Linguarum comparativa*, collected and published by command of the late Empress of Russia, in 2 vols. 4to.

RUSSIAN 2.

The Lord's Prayer, as used at the present day in the public service of the church in Russia.

Russian 3.

Otshe nash ije esi na nebesech. Da svetitsia imia tvoie. Da pridet tzarstvie tvoie. Da budet volia tvoia iako na nebesi i na zemli. Chleb nash nasuschnii dajid nam dnies. J ostavinam dolgi nasha jakoje i mi ostavliaem doljinicom nashim. J ne vovedi nas vo iscuschenie. No izbavi nas ot lucavago. Amen.

Samaritan 1.

hh z v h d g b a

aa s n m l k i th

t sch r q ts p

Samaritan 2.

hh z v h d g b a

aa s n m l k i th

t sch r q ts p

Russian 3.

The literal reading of the Lord's Prayer.

Orat. Dom. Amst. p. 78.

Samaritan 1.

The authors who have engaged in the dispute respecting the priority of the Hebrew and Samaritan alphabets, have been mentioned under the former article, (which see.) It is scarcely possible at this time to determine, whether alphabets were first used in Chaldea or Phenicia; but there can be little doubt, that the latter furnished letters to a far greater number of languages than the former. There is reason to believe that the Samaritan continued a living language for many centuries.

Fournier calls this *Idumean*, and says it was used by many nations in Asia, Vol. 2. p. 279. Duret says it was brought from the Levant, p. 324.

Samaritan 2.

This character is said to have been delineated after the course and movements of nature, Duret, p. 323.

Samaritan 3.

Samaritan 4.

Samaritan 5.

hh z v e d g b a

aa s n m l k i th

t sch r q ts p

SAMARITAN 3.

This character is also said, by Theseus Ambrosius, to have been formed from the same as the preceding; it was approved and received into use at Rome, and called ancient Greek.

Duret, p. 324.
Le Clabart, p. 517.

SAMARITAN 4.

This curious alphabet was taken from Samaritan coins by Walton.

Spanh. Dissert. p. 80.

SAMARITAN 5.

This alphabet is copied from

Encyc. Franc. pl. I.

Samaritan 6.

Samaritan 7.

Saracen 1.

SAMARITAN 6.

The modern Samaritan alphabet, copied by the late Dr. Morton, from a manuscript in the Cottonian library in the British Museum, and was by him esteemed the most correct of any extant.

Dr. Morton's Table.

SAMARITAN 7.

The Lord's Prayer, the literal reading of which is the same as the Hebrew.

Orat. Dom. p. 10.

SARACEN 1.

This character, according to Theseus Ambrosius, was used by the Saracens at the time of their conquests.

Duret, p. 475.

Saracen 2.

Saracen 3.

reh he ez tech te b a ayn

dgh ta cda sad sch za nun dal

mym la lam caph khab fl la vua

Saracen 4.

hh z v h d g b a

aa s n m l k i th

t sh r q ts p

SARACEN 2.

This alphabet is handed to us on the authority of John Baptist Palatin, a Roman citizen, in a learned treatise, "teaching to write in all languages and letters, both an-" cient and modern.

Duret, p. 475.

SARACEN 3.

Duret gives this alphabet as a Saracen, which seems to have some affinity to the Arabic. See this author, "De " la comparaison du scavoir Arabesque et Sarrasinesque, " avec l'Egyptien, Chaldaique, &c." p. 477.

SARACEN 4.

On the authority of Kircher this alphabet is given in Dr. Morton's Table.

SARACEN 5.

SARDINIAN 1.

Pare nostru, qui istas in sos quelos, siat sanctificadu su nomen teu: vengat à nois su regnu teu. Fasase sa voluntat tua, axi comen su quelu, gasi en la terra. Lo pa nostru de dognia die da nos hoc, I dexia à nos altres sos depitos nostros, comente nos ateros dexiam als deppitores nostros. Ino nos induescas in sa tentatio: mas livra nos de male. Amen.

SARDINIAN 2.

Babbu nostru, sughale ses in sos chelus: santufiada su nomine tuo: bengiad su rennu tuo: faciad si sa voluntade tua, comenti en chelo, gasi in sa terra. Su pane nostru de ogniedie da nos lu hoæ, et lassa à nosateros is deppidos nostrus, gasi comente è nosateros lassaos à sos deppidores nostrus. E non nos portis in sa tentassione. Impero libera nos da male. Amen.

SARACEN 5.

Inscription upon a bridge near the pyramids of Memphis.

Norden's Antiquities, Vol. 1. pl. 44.

SARDINIAN 1 and 2.

The Sardinians had formerly a language proper to themselves, but having past by conquests, under different governments, it has been considerably altered and corrupted; nevertheless it has retained many words not in any other tongue.

There are two principal languages spoken in this island; one of which is used in the cities and towns, and has a good deal of the Latin and Spanish in it, and is the No. 1. annexed. The other, which is the native tongue, is spoken in the country.

Duret, p. 818.

Savanna.

Keelah nossé kitshah awé heyring. Yah zong seway ononteeo. Agow aygon awoanneeo.—Yes yaon onang ché owah itsché heyring. Kaat shiack mowatgi hee kannaterow tyenteron. Esh keinong cha haowi eto neeot shkeynong haïtshé kitsha haowi. Ga ri waah et kaïn. Isse he owain matchi: Agow aigon issé sha waneeo egawain onaïng. Neeo.

Savoo.

A man	*Momonne*	The head	*Càtoo*
A woman	*Mobunne*	The hair	*Row càtoo*
A boy	*Monecopai*	Temples	*Otaïle*
A horse	*Dejaro*	The eyes	*Madda*
A hog	*Vavee*	The ears	*Wodeèloo*
A goat	*Kesàvoo*	The nose	*Sivànga*
A sheep	*Doomba*	The chin	*Pàgavee*
A boat	*Cova*	One	*Isse, ussc*
The sun	*Lodo*	Two	*Rooe*
The moon	*Wurroo*	Three	*Tulloo*
The sky	*Leèroo*	Four	*Uppa*
Smoke	*Sabooai*	Five	*Lumee*
Cold	*Mireèngee*	Six	*Unna*
Heat	*Kibàsoo*	Seven	*Petoo*
Fire	*Ace*	Eight	*Aroo*
Water	*Ailei*	Nine	*Saïo*
The earth	*Vorai*	Ten	*Singooroo*

SAVANNA.

This is the Lord's Prayer in the native language of Savanna in Georgia, in America.

Orat. Dom. Amst. p. 89.

SAVOO.

Taken from the vocabulary of the language of this island.

Parkinson's Voy. p. 163.

Saxon 1.

A	B	C	D	E	F	G	H
a	b	c	d	e	f	g	h
J	K	L	M	N	O	P	C
i	k	l	m	n	o	p	cu
R	S	T	Ð	V	X	Y	Z
r	s	t	dh	u	x	y	z

Saxon 2.

Aa Bb Cc Dꝺ Ðð Ee Fꝼ Gᵹ

Þh Iı Kk Ll Mm Nn Oo Pp

Rꞃ Sꞅ Tꞇ Wƿ Xx Yẏ Zz

Saxon 3.

Faꝺeꞃ vꞃen ðu aꞃð ın Þeoꝼnaꞅ, ꞅıe ᵹehal-ᵹuꝺ Noma ðın ꞇo cẏmeð ꞃıc ðın. ꞅıe ꝼıllo ðın ꞅuæ ıꞅ ın Þeoꝼne ⁊ ın Eoꞃða. Þlaꝼ uꝼ-eꞃne oꝼeꞃƿıꞅꞇlıc ꞅel uꞅ ꞇo ꝺæᵹ, ⁊ ꝼoꞃᵹeꝼ uꞅ ꞅcẏlða uꞃna ꞅuæ ƿe ꝼoꞃᵹeꝼon Scẏlᵹum uꞃum. Anꝺ ne ınleaꝺ uꞅıð ın Coꞅꞇnunᵹe, Ah ᵹeꝼꞃıᵹuꞅıch ꝼꞃom Evıl.

Saxon 1.

The form of this letter, at the time of the Saxon invasion, about the year 450, according to Gibson's chronicle, seems to have been quite unknown; but Dr. Johnson thinks this people were so illiterate, as most probably to have been without any alphabet.

The annexed, which is the most ancient Saxon character, is taken from

Dr. Morton's Table.

Saxon 2.

The modern Saxon alphabet, cast at the Type-Street Letter Foundery.

Saxon 3.

What the Saxon tongue was, long before the conquest, may be observed in the most ancient manuscript of that language, being a gloss on the Evangelists, by Eadfride, eighth bishop of Lindffarne, about A. D. 700, from which the annexed is taken.

Camden's Remains, p. 23.

Saxon 4.

Fæder ure þu þe earþ on heofenum, si þin nama Gehalgod to be cume þin rice; geƿurþe þin ƿilla on eorþan sƿa sƿa on heofenum, urne ge dæghƿanlican hlaf sýle us to dæg. And forgýf us ure gýltas, sƿa sƿa ƿe forgivaþ urum gýltendum. And ne gelædde þu us on costnung. Ac Alýse us of ýfle.

Saxon 5.

Thu ure fader þe eart on heofenum. Si þin nama gehalgod. Cum þin ric. Si þin ƿilla on eorþen, sƿa sƿa on heofenum. Sýle us to dæg urn dægƿanlican hlaf. And forgif us ure gýltas, sƿa sƿa ƿe forgifaþ þam þe ƿið us agýltaþ. And ne led þe us on costnung. Ac alýs us from ýfle. Si it sƿa.

Saxon 6.

Fader ure þu þe in heofnum earþ, beo gehalgud þin Noma. Cume to þin rice, ƿeorþe þin Ƿilla sƿa sƿa on Þeofune sƿile on eorþe. Ƿlaf ufenne dæghƿainlieu sel us to dæg, ⁊ forlete us ure Scýlde, sƿa sƿa ƿe ec forleten þaem þe Scýldigat ƿið us; geleade in Costnungæ, Ah gelefe us of Yfle.

Saxon 4.

The annexed Lord's Prayer is said to have been translated by King Alfred, A. D. 875.

Wilk Ess. p. 7.

Saxon 5.

The annexed is also the Lord's Prayer, from *Lisle's Saxon Monuments*, A. D. 900.

Wilk. Ess. p. 7.

Saxon 6.

This is taken from the Saxon homilies about the same date, and is called Dano-Saxon.

Martin's Inst. p. 14.

Saxon 7.

Faꝺeꞃ me þe aꞃꞇ ın heoꝼone, ꞅẏ ᵹebleꞇꞅob name þın, ꞅƿa ꞅƿa on heoꝼone anꝺ on eaꞃþan, bꞃeoꝺ uꞃe ꝺeᵹƿamlıch ᵹeoꝼ uꞅ ꞇo ꝺæᵹ, anꝺ ꝼoꞃᵹeoꝼ uꞅ aᵹelꞇeꞅ uꞃa ꞅƿa ꞅƿa ƿe ꝼoꞃᵹeoꝼen aᵹılꞇenꝺum mum. Ænꝺ ne leꝺ uꞅ on Coꞅꞇnunᵹe, an alẏꞅ uꞅ ꝼꞃom ẏꝼle. Sƿa beo hıꞇ.

Saxon 8.

Fæꝺeꞃ uꞃe þuþe ın heoꞅunum eaꞃð, beo ᵹehalᵹaꝺ þın noma; cume ꞇo þın ꞃıce, ƿeoꞃðe þın ƿılla ꞅƿa on heoꝼune ꞅƿılce on eoꞃðe. hlaꝼ uꞅeꞃne ꝺæᵹhƿæmlıce ꞅel uꞅ ꞇo ꝺæᵹe. ⁊ ꝼoꞃleꞇ uꞅ uꞃe ꞅcẏlꝺe ꞅƿæ ꞅƿæ ƿe ec ꝼoꞃleꞇen þæn þe ꞅcẏlꝺıᵹaꞇ ƿıð uꞅ. ⁊ ne ᵹelaeꞇ uꞅ ᵹelaeꝺe ın conꞅꞇunᵹæ, ah ᵹeleꞅe uꞅ oꝼ ẏꝼl

Saxon 9.

Fæꝺeꞃ uꞅeꞃ ꞅe þe ıꞅ on heoꝼnum, ᵹıhalᵹoꝺ bıð noma ðın, ꞇo cẏmeð ꞃıce þın, ꞅıe ƿılla þın ꞅıe ꞅƿa on heoꝼne ⁊ on eaꞃðo, hlaꝼ uꞅeꞃne ꝺæᵹhƿæmlıce ꞅel uꞅ ꞇo ꝺæᵹe, ⁊ ᵹoꞃꞅᵹeꝼ uꞅ ꞅẏnne uꞅe ꞅƿa ꝼæꞅꞇlıce ⁊ ec he ꝼoꞃᵹeoꝼaꞅ eᵹhƿelce ꞅcẏlꝺe uꞅeꞃ, ⁊ ne uꞃıh on læꝺ ðu ın coꞅꞇunᵹe, ah aꝼꞃıa uꞃıh ꝼꞃom.

Saxon 7.

The Lord's Prayer, from the Psalter of Trinity college, A. D. 1130, in the time of King Stephen.

Martin's Inst. p. 14.

Saxon 8.

Another version of the Lord's Prayer, from the Rushworth library.

Orat. Dom. Amst. p. 57.

Saxon 9.

This version of the same is also taken from the Rushworth library.

Orat. Dom. Amst. p. 58.

Schwabacher.

Aa Bb Cc Dd Ee Ff Gg Hh Iij

Kk Ll Mm Nn Oo Pp Qq Rrꝛ Sſs ß

Tt Uu Vv Xx Yy Zz Ww. ß ck fi ff

Sclavonian 1.

Sclavonian 2.

Oche nash izghæ yease nanæbæsægh, da sueatesa ima tuoæ, da predet tzaazstuia tuoæ, da boodet volya tuoya yaco na nebesæ inazemle. Ghlœb nash nasou schneei dazgd nam dnæs. Jo staue nam dolghii nasha yaco imwee ostavelayem dolzgnecom nashim. Ineuedi nas fpapast. No jzbaue nas ot loocauaho. Amen.

Schwabacher.

So named from the town of Schwabach in Franconia, where it was invented about the year 1500, and was at one time much in use in Germany.

Fourn. v. 2. p. 267.

Sclavonian 1.

Many nations, both in Europe and Asia, speak this language; it is used generally in all the eastern parts of Europe, except Greece, Hungary, and Wallachia; but these nations have a variety of characters.

Fourn. v. 2. p. 226.

Sclavonian 2.

The Lord's Prayer.

Wilk. Ess. p. 435.
Orat. Dom. p. 24.

SCLAVONIAN 3.

Otsse nass, ki yessi na nebessi. Ssuhtisse ime tuoie. Pridi kralyeusstuo, budi uolia tuoia, kako na nebu ina zemlij. Kruha nassega ssagdanigad ai namga danass, I odpusciainam dughe nasse, kako i mi odpusciamo dusuikon nassijm, I nepeliai nats u napast, da izbaui nats od nepriazni. Amen.

SCOTS 1.

Our fader, vhilk ar in hevin: hallovit be thy name: thy kingdon cum: thy vil be doin in erth, as it is in hevin. Gif uss yijs day our daily bred, and forgif us our sinnis, as we forgif them that sin agains us. Et led us not into tentation: bot delyver us from evil. Amen.

SCOTS 2.

Ar nathairne ata ar neamh, goma beannuigte hainmsa, gu deig do rioghachdsa, dentaa do iholfi air dtalmhuin mar ata air neamh, tabhair dhuinn anuigh ar naran laitheamhuil, agas maith dhuinn ar bhfiacha, amhuil mhathmuid dar bhfeicheamhnuibh, agas na leig ambuadhread sinn, achd saor sinn o olc. Oir is leatsa an rioghachd an cumhachd agas an gloir gu siorraidh. Amen.

SCLAVONIAN 3.

Another reading of the Lord's Prayer.

Duret, p. 744.
Orat. Dom. p. 59.

SCOTS 1.

The Lord's Prayer used in the Lowlands of Scotland.

Orat. Dom. p. 56.

SCOTS 2.

The Lord's Prayer of the Highlands of Scotland, which appears to be the Celtic or Gaelic.

Orat. Dom. Amst. p. 49.

Servian 1.

Servian 2.

Servian 3.

a b v g d e ch z

z i td i y k l m

n x ŏ p r s t u

v f h ps ō sct cz c

Servian 1. and 2.

These are the characters used in the most eastern parts of Europe, and are said to have been invented by St. Jerome.

Duret, p. 733.

Servian 3.

This alphabet is attributed to St. Cyrillus, and, like the above, is used in the eastern parts of Europe. It was invented about the year 700.

Fourn. v. 2. p. 275.
Encyc. Franc. pl. XI.

Servian 4.

Otse nash ishe jeszi v nabeszih, poszueti sze ime tvoje, pridi kralesztvo tvoje, budi volya tvoja kako v nebi tako i na zemli, hlib nash ushakdanni dai nan danasz, j odpuszti nam duge nashe kako i mi odpusztamo dushnikom nashim, j ne vovedi nasz v napaszt, da izbavi nasz odi zla; jako tvoje je kralesztvo i mocz i zava na veki. Amen.

Siamic 1.

ko khò khó khò khoo ngo cho sò

do to thó no bo ppó fo yo

ro lo vo so só hò o kâ

Siamic 2.

Po raou you savang, scheu pra hai prakot touk heng kon tang tai: touai pra pon. Meuang pra co hai dai ke raou. Hai leou ning tchai pra meuang pen-din semo savang. Ahan raou touk van co hai dai ke raou van ni. Coprot bap raou, semo raou prot pou tam bap ke raou, ya hai raou tok nai kouan bap. Hai poun kiac anerai tang-poang. Amen.

SERVIAN 4.

The Lord's Prayer.

Orat. Dom. Amst. p. 81.

SIAMIC 1.

The language of Siam partakes much of the Chinese, the words being almost all monosyllables.

This alphabet is taken from

Encyc. Franc. pl. XXI.

SIAMIC 2.

The Lord's Prayer.

Orat. Dom. p. 32.

Siamic 3.

Poo orao giou sowen; thiou pra hai pra chot tob hayn con tang laë tovaë pra pon moang, pra cob hay daë kie rao, haë leo neung kiaë pra mogan hain din somoë souän. Ha ha rao toub van coo haë duë kéé prao van nyy, coo prot bap rao semoe rao prot pouou tam kéé rao, gaa haë prao top naë coang bap, haë

Siberian.

Otjé mitsjé kandi koendsjoenga, temlælængh nim totlie, legatei poegandallanpoh totlie, læ-tiot t'sjemol alkaltei konda koedzjuga je levi-anh, lunliagel miltje monidetjelæh keyck mi-tin telaman, jeponkatsi mitin taldelpon mïtlæ poel mïtkondan poniatsjok tannevinol mitlæ-poel, je kondo dgonilæk mïtel olo olmïk, kon

Spanish 1.

Padre nuestro, que estas en los cielos, sanctifi-cado sea el tu nombre; venga à nos el tu rey-no: fagase tu voluntad, assi en la tierra, como en el cielô. El pan nuestro de cada dia da nos lo oy: y perdona nos nuestras deudas, assi co-mo nostros perdonamos à nuestros deudores. Y no nos dexes caër en la tentation: mas li-bra nos de mal; porgue tuyo es el reyno, y la potentia, y la gloria, por todos los siglos. Am.

Siamic 3.

The Lord's Prayer.

Orat. Dom. Amst. p. 22.

Siberian.

The reading of the Lord's Prayer, from a manuscript in my possession, taken from Witsius's Description of Tartary.

Spanish 1.

The Lord's Prayer, from the New Testament in this language, Amst. 1625.

Wilk. Ess. p. 435

Spanish 2.

Padre nuestro que estas en los cielos, sanctificado sea tu nombre, venga tu reyno, hagase tu volontad assi en la tierra como en el cielo, danos hoy nuestro pan cotidiano; y perdona nos nuestras deudas assi como nos otros perdonamos à nuestros deudores, y no nos metas en tentacion, mas libra nos de mal, porque tuyo es el reyno y la potencia &c. Amen.

Spanish 3.

Padre nuestro que estás en el cielo, sanctificado sea tu nombre; venga nos tu reyno: hagase tu voluntad, assi en la tierra como en el cielo; el pan nuestro de cada dia dá nos le oy; y perdona nos nuestras deudas assi como nosotros perdonamos á nuestros deudores; y no nos dexes caer en tentacion, mas libra nos de mal. Amen.

Swedish 1.

Fader war som ast i himmelen, helgat warde titt nampn; till komme titt ricke, skei tin wilie sa pa jordenne som i himmelen: wart dagliga brod giff oss i dagh; och forlat oss wara skulder sa som ock wi forlaten them oss skyldege aro: och in leed oss icke i frestelse; ut an frals oss i fra ondo. Tii riiket ar titt, och ma-

SPANISH 2.

Another reading of the Lord's Prayer.

Orat. Dom. Amst. p. 45.

SPANISH 3.

The reading of the Lord's Prayer in modern Spanish, communicated to me by a learned gentleman.

SWEDISH 1.

The Lord's Prayer, from a bible in this language, Stockh. 1674.

Wilk. Ess. p. 435.

Swedish 2.

Fader war, som äst i himmelen, helgadt warde titt namn: tilkomme titt rike: ske tin wilje, sasom i himmelen, sa ock pa jorden: gif oss i dag wart dageliga bröd: och forlat oss wara skulder, sasom ock wi förlate them oss skyldige äro: ock inled oss icke i frestelse, utan frals oss ifran ondo: ty riket är titt och magten och härligheten i ewighet. Amen.

Syriac 1.

ܚ	ܙ	ܘ	ܗ	ܕ	ܓ	ܒ	ܐ
hh	z	v	h	d	g	b	a
ܥ	ܣ	ܢ	ܡ	ܠ	ܟ	ܝ	ܛ
aa	s	n	m	l	k	i	th
ܬ	ܫ	ܪ	ܩ	ܨ	ܦ		
t	sch	r	q	ts	p		

Syriac 2.

ܚ	ܙ	ܘ	ܗ	ܕ	ܓ	ܒ	ܐ
hh	z	v	h	d	g	b	a
ܥ	ܣ	ܢ	ܡ	ܠ	ܟ	ܝ	ܛ
ee	s	n	m	l	k	j	th
ܬ	ܫ	ܪ	ܩ	ܨ	ܦ		
t	sch	r	q	ss	p		

Swedish. 2.

This copy of the Lord's Prayer, as now used in Sweden, was given to me by my friend the Rev. S. Nisser, minister to the Swedish congregation, East Smithfield.

Syriac.

This language is one of those several dialects, commonly called the Oriental tongues, and is pretended to have been the mother of them all. It became a distinct tongue so early as the days of Jacob; for what his father in law and uncle, Laban, of *Padan-aram* or *Mesopotamia*, calls *Jegar-sahadutha*, is, by Jacob, called *Galeed.* The Syriac was not only the language of *Syria*, but also of *Mesopotamia*, *Chaldea;* for there is no more difference between the *Chaldean* and *Syriac*, than between the English and Scots; *Assyria*, and after the Babylonish captivity, *Palestine*.

There are three dialects of the *Syrian* tongue; first, the *Aramean*, or *Syriac*, properly so called, which is the most elegant, and used in *Mesopotamia*, by the inhabitants of *Roha*, or *Edessa*, and *Harran*, and the outer *Syria*: second, the dialect of Palestine, spoken by the inhabitants of Damascus, Mount Libanus, and the inner *Syria:* third, the *Chaldean* or *Nabathean* dialect, the most rude and unpolished of the three, and used in the mountainous parts of *Assyria*, and in the villages of *Irak* or *Babylonia*.

The Syriac character is very ancient, and supposed, by some, to have been in use above 300 years B. C.

There is a number of books written in this language, very little known to the Europeans; but what this tongue is most to be valued for, are the excellent translations therein of the Old and New Testament; which equal, if they do not surpass, those of any other language.

Universal Hist. Vol. 1. p. 377.

Syriac 1.

Duret gives this as the most ancient Hebrew character, and intimates that it was used both by Abraham and Moses. P. 364.

Syriac 2.

This is the Stranghelo, or ancient Chaldean, long since gone out of use; the Lord's Prayer is to be seen in this character in the second volume of the Propaganda in my possession.

The annexed was copied from

Castellus's Lexicon, Vol. 1. p. 2.

Syriac 3.

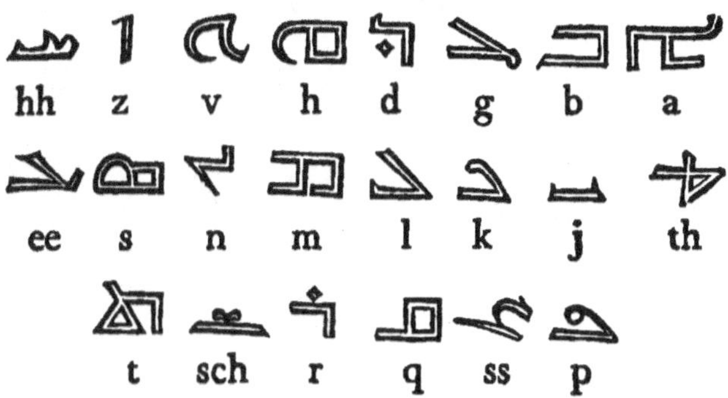

Syriac 4.

Syriac 5.

hh z v h d g b a

aa s n m l k i th

t sh r q ts p

Syriac 3.

The Stranghelo character, called *Duplex;* but no mention is made of it's use.

Castell. Lex. Vol. 1. p. 2.

Syriac 4.

Called *Nestorian.* These Syrians were spread over Tartary about the twelfth century, whence they established missions.

Castell. Lex. Vol. 1. p. 2.

Syriac 5.

This is also a Nestorian.

Encyc. Franc. pl. 2.

Syriac 6.

hh z v h d g b a

aa s n m l k i th

t sch r q ts p

Syriac 7.

hh z v h d g b a

aa s n m l k i th

t sh r q ts p

Syriac 8.

Abhoun dbhaschmajo. Nethkadasch schmoch Tithe malchouthoch. Nehve zebjonoch, ajchano dbhaschmajo, oph b'ar'ho. Habh lan lach mo dsunkonan jaumono. Vaschbouk lan chav bain, ajchano d'oph chnan schbhakan l'chajobhain. V'lo ta'alan lnesjouno. Elo pazan men bischo. Metül ddiloch hi malchoutho v'chajlo, v'theschbouchtho l'olam ol'min.

Syriac 6.

Duret, p. 365, says, that this alphabet is composed of small, or running letters, with which the Syrians write more freely on account of their joining.

Syriac 7.

This is the modern alphabet, as used in printing at this day.

Syriac 8.

The literal reading of the Lord's Prayer, from a new testament in this language, Hamb. 1663.

Orat. Dom. p. 12.

Syriac 9.

Abûn dbhascmaja: netquadasch scmoch: thethe malkuthoch: nehva zebjonoch aikano dbhascmaja apf barêa hablan lahhma dsûnquonan jaumona: wasebûk lân hhaubain vehhatthin, aikana dapf hhnan scbaquan lehhaibhin: welah thelan lenishjûna: elah fatsah menbisca mettul dedihloch hih malkutta wehhaila wetescbuhhta leehlam ehlmin. Amin.

Syro-Galilean.

hh z v h d g b a

aa s n m l k i th

t sh r q ts p

Syro-Hebraic.

hh z v h d g b a

s n n m l k i th

t sh r q ts p aa

Syriac 9.

The reading of the Lord's Prayer in the Stranghelo style.
Orat. Dom. Amst. p. 6.

Syro-Galilean.

This is more properly called an ancient Chaldean, and is said to have been used by some oriental christians, calling themselves disciples of John the Baptist. They inhabited the city of Bassora and its environs.

Encyc. Franc. pl. VII.

Syro-Hebraic.

This character was much used formerly by the Jews in Syria.

Fourn. Vol. 2. p. 227.

Sumatran.

One	*Chit*	Two	*Nung*
Three	*Sa*	Four	*See*
Five	*Ingo*	Six	*La*
Seven	*Chee*	Eight	*Poë*
Nine	*Ca*	Ten	*Tsap*
The sun	*Jet*	A man	*Tapò*
The moon	*Geuex*	A woman	*Tsawà*
The stars	*Tchee*	The head	*Taow*
The sky	*Thee*	The hair	*Tamung*
Rain	*Hò*	The face	*Beeïn*
The sea	*Haï*	The eyes	*Bwaclieu*
Wind	*Whang*	The nose	*Pee*

Tartaric 1.

يا بابامز كه يوكسك ڭوڭده سن
آدڭ آري اولسون
پادشاهلغڭ ڭلسون
بويرقلرڭ اتمش اولسون ڭوڭده كبي
دخي يرده
هر ڭونڭي اكمكموزي وير بيزه بو ڭون
و بورجلرمزي بيزه بغشله نتكم بيز دخي
بورجلولرمزي بغشلرز
و بيزي صينشه ڭتورمه
لكن يرمزدن بيزي صالي ويز [او قورتر و
صقله]

SUMATRAN.

This specimen of the language is taken from Sidney Parkinson's Voyage, p. 198, and is very different from the vocabulary of tongues used in this island, given by W. Marsden, Esq. p. 168 of his work, and which my reader will find in the appendix, under the names of ACHEEN, BATTA, REJANG, and LAMPOON.

TARTARIC 1.

The Tartaric alphabet in general use is the Arabic. The annexed specimen is the Lord's Prayer.

Orat. Dom. p. 19.

Tartaric 2.

Ya Atámùz ki yûksèk ghiôghdá sen, aadin âri olsoun, pâdishâh-líghin ghelsoun, boiruklérin itmish olsoun ghiôghda kibì dahi yírda, herghiûnaghi ekmekimúzi vîr bizè bû-ghiûn, va bourgilerimúzi bizè baghíshla nítakim biz dahi bourgilulerimúzi baghishlériz, va bizì siníshа ghiturmà, lakìn yaramazdàn bizì sáli-vir, zirá-ki senúngh-dur padishah-lìk va kadirlìk.

Tartaric 3.

Jez mé koendind jejand nopkon, noeni nip tät, tule noetkotsi tät, tät ténel tät tät nopkon its jots jogodt, nai mé tsjelelemi tallel mekosjek titap, kvodtsjedi mekosjek kolzja mei, tät mei kvodtsjedi kolzja mei, nick jgosjid kvondik mat kekend, tät mat losogod; tät tät noedkotsi oroep oevorganin tam noen. Nat.

Tartaric 4.

Abcade thégé megni ama. Sini kebou endouringhe okini. Sini couron tchikini. Nade abcade adali sini couninde atchaboukini. Jnenghitari i tchecou enenhhi mende poureou, kéli kerenni ëndeboucoubé megni couë'bouréou. Kéli membé pouyendé oume togimbouré. Elemanga membe egetchi tchaïlabouréou.— Ere sonkoi okini.

Tartaric 2.

The literal reading of the preceding Lord's Prayer.

Orat. Dom. p. 19.

Tartaric 3.

The reading of the Lord's Prayer of the Ostiak Tartars, from Witsius's description of Tartary, Vol. 2. p. 633, of which I have a correct MS. copy.

Tartaric 4.

Another reading of the Lord's Prayer in the Chinese stile.

Orat. Dom. Amst. p. 13.

Tartaric 5.

pa pa ka na ou ou o i e a

ra khe ya ts ts ma la tha sca sa

sci se tche tchi ja tsa tca fa oüa

Tartaric 6.

pa pa ka na ou ou o i e a

ra khe ya ts ts ma la tha sca sa

sci se tche tchi ja tsa tca fa oüa

Tartaric 7.

pa pa ka na ou ou o i e a

ra khe ya ts ts ma la tha sca sa

sci se tche tchi ja tsa tca fa oüa

Tartaric 5.

The Mantcheou Tartars use the same alphabet or characters as those of the Great Mogul, and write them from top to bottom, after the manner of the Chinese.

The annexed is a specimen of the initial letters.

Encyc. Franc. pl. XXIII.

Tartaric 6.

A specimen of the medial letters of the alphabet of the Mantcheou Tartars.

Encyc. Franc. pl. XXIII.

Tartaric 7.

A specimen of the final letters of the alphabet of the Mantcheou Tartars.

Encyc. Franc. pl. XXIII

TALENGA.

అ	ఆ	ఇ	ఈ	ఉ	ఊ	ఋ	ౠ
ă	ā	ĭ	ī	oŭ	oū	roŭ	roū

ఌ	ౡ	ఎ	ఐ	ఒ	ఔ	అం	అః
loŭ	loū	e	aï	o	aou	au	âha

క	ఖ	గ	ఘ	ఙ	చ	ఛ	జ
ka	k'ha	ga	g'ha	nga	tcha	tcha	ja

ఝ	ఞ	ట	ఠ	డ	ఢ	ణ	త	థ
j'ha	igna	ta	t'ha	da	d'ha	na	ta	t'ha

ద	ధ	న	ప	ఫ	బ	భ	మ	య
da	d'ha	na	pa	p'ha	ba	b'ha	ma	ya

ర	ల	వ	శ	ష	స	హ	ళ	క్ష
ra	lạ	oa	chā	chă	sa	ha	la	k'chạ

TAMOULIC.

க	ங	ச	ஞ	ட	ண	த	ந
kă	nă	scha	gna	da	na	ta	na

ப	ம	ய	ர	ல	வ	ழ	ள
pạ	mặ	ja	rặ	la	vă	ra	la

ற	ன
rra	na

Talenga.

This is the alphabet of a province of the powerful kingdom of Decan, in India; the language is vulgarly called *Badega*. In the French library is a grammar and other books in this tongue.

Encyc. Franc. pl. XIX.

Tamoulic.

This is also called *Malabaric*, and has been usually written on palm-leaves with a pointed tool, but it is now much in use in India in letter-press printing.

This radical alphabet is taken from

Encyc. Franc. pl. XIX.

Tchoka.

The eyes	*Chi*	Eyebrows	*Tara*
Forehead	*Quechetan*	Nose	*Etou*
Mouth	*Tsara*	Teeth	*Yma*
Tongue	*Aon*	Beard	*Téhé*
Back	*Saitourou*	Belly	*Hone*
Fire	*Houncohi*	A dog	*Tamoui*
The sun	*Tsouhou*	The wind	*Tébaira*
Yes	*He, hi*	No	*Hya*
To eat	*Ajbe*	To drink	*Cbuka*
To sleep	*Etaro*	To snore	*Mouaro*
The hair	*Chapa*	The arms	*Tacts sonk*
The wrist	*Tay-ha*	The hand	*Tay pompé*
The sea	*Tchoiza*	A ship	*Kaïani*
A bow	*Couhon*	A needle	*Kaine*
A feather	*Qs-lari*	A fly	*Omoch*
A musket	*Taipo*	A cabin	*Pouhau*

Thibetan.

ཀ་	ཁ་	ག་	ང་།	ཅ་	ཆ་	ཇ་	ཉ་།
kha	kha	k	ngha	ciha	ciha	cia	gnia
ཏ་	ཐ་	ད་	ན་།	པ་	ཕ་	བ་	མ་།
tha	tha	ta	na	pha	pha	pa	ma
ཙ་	ཚ་	ཛ་	ཝ་།	ཞ་	ཟ་	འ་	ཡ་།
tzha	tzha	tza	va	sciha	sa	ha	ja
ར་	ལ་	ཤ་	ས་།	ཧ་	ཨ་།		
ra	la	scia	sa	hah	aa		

TCHOKA.

This specimen is copied from the vocabulary of the language, in

Pérouse, Vol. 2. p. 488.

THIBETAN.

The alphabet of the Lamas of Thibet, taken from the second volume of the Propaganda Fide.

Teutonic 1.

Teutonic 2.

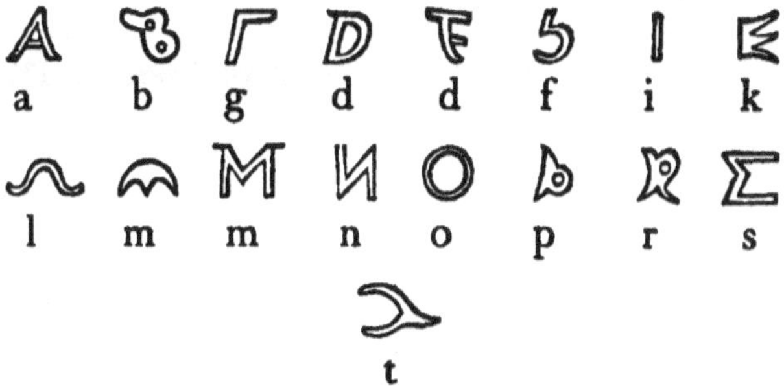

Tungusian.

Aminmoen moengi avagoe negdaoegidadoe. Garisjegan gerbisch singi. Jemesjegal ogdigoe singi. Osjegan sitlu singi on negdadoe do endradoe. Kiltere moengi inegdoe boekal moendoe tikin. Akakal moendoe ogbi moengi on boe amnenkiteref kotatsjaldoe moendoeck.— Aminkalivra moendoe jeregdoevi. A jikal moendoe malgadoeck. On sin gi bisin ogdidgoe mandi baschin jereger. Tésje.

Teutonic 1.

This alphabet was taken from an ancient manuscript in the cathedral of Wurtzberg, in Franconia.

Fourn. Vol. 2. p. 272.

Teutonic 2.

This alphabet is taken from

Encyc. Britan. pl. IX.

Tungusian.

The reading of the Lord's Prayer, from Witsius's description of Tartary.

Orat. Dom. Amst. p. 14.

Turkish 1.

بيزوم اتامز كه كوكلرده سين ،

سنك ادك مقدس اولسون ،

سنك ملكوتك كلسون

سنك ارادتك اولسون نته كيم كوكده

دخي يرده ،

هركونكي بيروم اتمكموزي وير بيره بو

كون ،

وبيزوم بورجلرومي بيره بغشله نته كيم بيز

دخي بيرزوم بورخلونرومزه بغشلرور ،

Turkish 2.

Bizoum atamuz kih gouglerdeh sin. Senun adun mukaddes olsoun. Senun melcoutun gel soun. Senun iradetun olsoun nitegim gougde dahi jerde. Hergoungi bizoum etmegemouzi ver bize bougioun. Vabisoum bourgsleroumi bize bagischle nitegim biz dahi bizoum bourgsloukeroumuze bagischlerouz. Vabisi tagsrib adchal etma. Lekin scherirden bizi ne-gsat eile. Zira senunder melcut vesultanet vemegs di ta ebed. Amin.

Turkish 1.

The Turkish alphabet is the same as the Arabic, No. 2, (which see) with the addition of five more letters.

The annexed is the Lord's Prayer in that character.

Orat. Dom. p. 18.

Turkish 2.

The literal reading of the above.

Orat. Dom. p. 18.

TYRIAN.

VIRGINIAN.

Nooshun kesukquot. Quittiana tamunach koowesuonk. Peyaumooutch kukketassootamóonk. Kuttenantamoónk nen nach ohkeit neane kesukquut. Nummeetsuongash asekesukokish assamaijneau yeuyeu kesukod. Kah ahquontamai inneau numat cheseongash neane matchenehu queagig nuta quonta mounonog Ah que sagkompaguna innean en qutchhua.

VANDAL.

Woschzi nasch kéns sy nunebv, nsvesche meno twojo, psiszknam kralostvo twojo, sestavi wola twoja yako nanebo ytu nazemi, kleb nasch dneisthi day nam schnisz. A wodai nam wini nashe, ak my wodawani winikom naszym, A newesich nas dopitowaine; Ale umosz nas od slego. Li.

Tyrian.

Fournier, Vol. 2. p. 274, calls this Tyrian, or Punic, but is silent as to any authority.

Virginian.

The reading of the Lord's Prayer.

Orat. Dom. p. 64.

Vandal.

The Lord's Prayer.

Orat. Dom. Amst. p. 80*.

Wallachian 1.

Tatul nostru csinye jesh in cseruj. Szvinczie sze numelye tuo. Sze vii imparaczia ta. Fii voja ta cum in cserui, asha shi pe pamuntul. Punye nostru de te zilelie da noi asztesz. Jarta greshalelye nostre cum shi noi jartam a greshitilor nostri. Shi nu ducs pe noi inka la iszpitira. Shi mentujeshte pe noi de ro. Amin.

Wallachian 2.

Parintye nostru csela cse jesh in cseri. Svenczie sze numelye tuo. Vii imparaczia ta. Facse sze voja ta cum in cseri asha shi pe pamuntul. Punye nostru csaszecsio da noo asztesz. Shi lasza noo datorilye nostre cum shi noi leszam datornicsilor nostri, shi nu ducs pe noi la iszpitira. Shi mentujeste pe noi de hitlyanul.

Waldenses.

Our narme ata air neamb'. Beanich atanim gu diga do riogda gu denta du hoill, air talm' in mar ta ar neamb' tabhar d'im an míigh ar naran limb' ail, agus mai d'uíne ar fiach ambail near marhmhid ar fiacha. Na leig si'n amb' aribh ach soarsa shin on. Ole or sletsa rioghta combta agns gloir gnsibhiri. Amen.

Wallachian 1 and 2.

These are two dialects of the Wallachian tongue, of which the reader may be the better judge, they being both given in the Lord's Prayer.

Orat. Dom. Amst. p. 77.

Waldenses.

This language appears to be the Celtic, and upon comparison with the Irish, and that of the Highlands of Scotland, will be found to be nearly the same.

The annexed is the Lord's Prayer.

Orat. Dom. Amst. p. 39.

WALLOON.

Pærinthele nostru cela ce esti en cheri. Svintzas cæse numele teu. Vie enperetziæ ta. Facæse voe ta, cum en tzer asesi pre pæmentu. Pæne noastre tza sætzioace dæ noaæ astezi. Si lase noaæ datorii le noastre, cum si noi se læsæm datornitzilor nostri. Si nu dutze preno i la ispitire: Tze ne mentueste prenoi de viclianul. Amin.

WELCH 1.

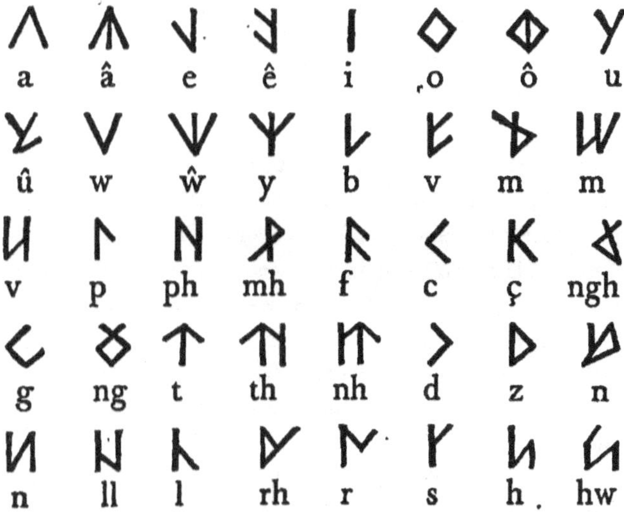

Walloon.

The reading of the Lord's Prayer.

Orat. Dom. p. 45.

Welch 1.

The alphabet of these primitive letters contains sixteen radical characters and powers, which have twenty-four secondary ones, modifications, or inflexions, making forty in all; and it went under the name of *Coelbren y Beirz*, the billet of signs of the Bards, or the Bardic Alphabet.

The discerning antiquary will naturally be desirous of knowing in what manner this curious relick was preserved to the present time: in reply to which; in the obscure and mountainous parts of Wales, the system of Bardism is still to be found entire, but more known to the world by the name of Druidism, which was properly that branch of Bardism relating to religion and education. *Bardism* was universal, and comprehended all the knowledge or philosophy of the ancient times; *Druidism* was it's religious code; and *Ovatism*, it's arts and sciences.

The preservation of the character may be principally attributed to it's own provision and means, whereby tradition is reduced to a science.

I am indebted for this and the following article to my ingenious friend W. Owen, F. A. S. whose authority cannot be doubted.

Welch 2.

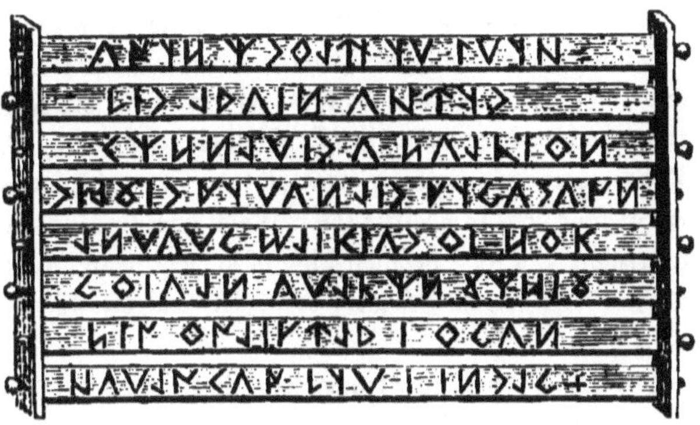

New Zealand.

One	*Katahè*	Father	*Papa*
Two	*Karooa*	Son	*Hetamàeh*
Three	*Katarroo*	The eyes	*He matta*
Four	*Kawha*	The nose	*He eih*
Five	*Kareema*	A dog	*Egoorree*
Six	*Kàònoo*	Fish	*Teyka*
Seven	*Kawhetoo*	Ear-shells	*Hepaooa*
Eight	*Kawarroo*	A stone	*Powhattoo*
Nine	*Kàeeva*	Water	*Hewai*
Ten	*Kacahaoro*	A house	*Hèàwhài*
A hedge	*Patéeà*	A nail	*Ewhàò*
A hatchet	*Kochee*	Victuals	*Eëi*
A garment	*Hecacahoo*	Tataow	*Emaho*
A canoe	*Hewaca*	To paddle	*Hoggee*
To speak	*Orero*	Good	*Apoorotoo*
Yes	*A a*	Bad	*Ekeeno*
No	*Kaowra*	Look you	*Eta eta*

WELCH 2.

The original manner of writing among the ancient Britons was by cutting the letters with a knife upon sticks, which were most commonly squared, and sometimes formed into three sides; consequently, a single stick contained either four or three lines. (See Ezekiel, ch. XXXVII, v. 16.) The squares were used for general subjects, and for stanzas of four lines in poetry; the trilateral ones were adapted to triades, and for a peculiar kind of ancient metre, called *Triban*, and *Englyn Milwyr*, or triplet, and the warriors' verse.

Several sticks, with writing upon them, were put together, forming a kind of frame, as represented in the annexed page, which was called *Peithynen*, or *Elucidator;* and was so constructed, that each stick might be turned for the facility of reading, the end of each running out alternately on both sides of the frame.

The following is a literal reading of this curious specimen in the modern orthography, with a correct translation.

Aryv y doeth yw pwyll:
Bid ezain alltud:
Cyvnewid â haelion:
Diengid rhywan eid rhygadarn:
Enwawg meiçiad o'i voç:
Goiaen awel yn nghyving:
Hir oreistez i ogan:
Llawer câr byw i Indeg.

TRANSLATION.

The weapon of the wise is reason.
Let the exile be moving.
Commerce with generous ones.
Let the very feeble run away; let the very powerful proceed.
The swincherd is proud of his swine.
A gale is almost ice in a narrow place.
Long penance to slander.
The frail Indeg has many living relations.

NEW ZEALAND.

Taken from the vocabulary of this language.

Parkinson's Voy. p. 126

ACHASTLIEN.

Moukala	Outis	Capes	Outiti	Is
1	2	3	4	5

Etesake	Kaleis	Oulousmarakhen	Pak	Tonta
6	7	8	9	10

ACHEEN.

One	*Sah*	Husband	*Lackaye*
Two	*Dua*	Wife	*Beenaye*
Three	*Tloo*	Father	*Bah*
Four	*Paat*	Mother	*Mau*
Five	*Leemung*	Head	*Oolou*
Six	*'Nam*	Eyes	*Matta*
Seven	*Taojoo*	Nose	*Eedoon*
Eight	*D'lappan*	Hair	*Oh*
Nine	*Sakoorang*	Teeth	*Geguy*
Ten	*Saploo*	Hand	*Jarrooay*
Day	*Ooraye*	Night	*Mallam*
White	*Pootee*	Black	*Hetam*
Die	*Mattay*	Good	*Gaet*
Fire	*Appooy*	Water	*Eer*
Cocoa nut	*Oo*	Rice	*Breeagh*

ACHASTLIEN.

A colony of North California. The numerous colonies which divide this country, although very near each other, live insulated, and have each a different language.

Annexed is the vocabulary of numeration, which alone is given, from the great difficulty of learning the tongue.

Pérouse, Vol. 2. p. 243.

ACHEEN.

This is one of the languages spoken in the island of Sumatra, taken from the comparative vobabulary.

Marsden, p. 168.

Batta 1.

Batta 2.

One	*Sadah*	Husband	*Morah*
Two	*Duo*	Wife	*Aboo*
Three	*Toloo*	Father	*Ammah*
Four	*Opat*	Mother	*Enang*
Five	*Leemah*	Head	*Ooloo*
Six	*Onam*	Eyes	*Mahtah*
Seven	*Paitoo*	Nose	*Aygong*
Eight	*Ooalloo*	Hair	*Oboo*
Nine	*Seeah*	Teeth	*Ningee*
Ten	*Sapooloo*	Night	*Borgning*
White	*Nabottar*	Black	*Naberong*
Die	*Mahtay*	Good	*Dengan*
Fire	*Ahpee*	Water	*Ayck*
Cocoa nut	*Crambee*	Rice	*Dahano*

Batta 1.

The alphabet of one of the principal internal languages of Sumatra.

Marsden, p. 168.

Batta 2.

This specimen of the Batta language, which is spoken in the island of Sumatra, is taken from the comparative vocabulary.

Marsden, p. 168.

Barman.

က	ခ	ဂ	ဃ	င	စ	ဆ	ဇ	ဈ	ဉ	ဋ
k	kh	g	gh	ng	z	zh	z	zh	gn	t
ဌ	ဍ	ဎ	ဏ	တ	ထ	ဒ	ဓ	န	ပ	ဖ
ch	d	dh	n	t	th	d	dh	n	p	ph
ဗ	ဘ	မ	ယ	ရ	လ	ဝ	သ	ဟ	ဠ	အ
b	bh	m	j	r	l	v	s	h	l	a

Bengallee.

Bappa kita, jang adda dė surga, Namma-mou jadi bersakti, radjat-mou mendarang, kand-hatimou menjadi de bumi seperti de surga, roti kita derri sa hari-hari membrikan kita sa hari inila, Makka ber-ampunla padakita doosa kita, seperti kita ber-ampun-akan siapa bersala kapada kita, d'jang-an hentar kita kapada tjobahan, tetapi lepasken kita dari jang d'jakat: karna mou pun'ja radjat daan kauwassahan daan berbessaran sampey kakakal. Amin.

Barman.

This alphabet is used in the kingdom of Ava; also in the island of Ceylon, a thousand miles distant, where it is called Cingalese.

The order and power of the letters are the same as the Nagari, (which see.)

The alphabet is copied from that celebrated work, the Propaganda, Vol. 1.

Bengallee.

The reading of the Lord's Prayer.

Orat. Dom. Amst. p. 23.

Courlandic.

Tews mûs kut tu esch in debbes. Sweérti to tau waêrtsch, Innēkas moms tau walstieb. Tau spraets noteék in debbes kavērssu semes. Mûs schjodēnysch to maisyd do tû moms schjod-eên. Pomettêes mus parradûs kames pommê-têm sau paradnēkem. Nêwét moms eck sch-jan. Laune kaedēnāeschjēn: Ais to tés tau walstybē, tau speax, tau gôetsch, tau musiga besgat. Omen.

Domesday.

Robt' ten' de ead fem' . *Criz* . Boln tenuit T.R.E. 7 geldb p dim' hida . Tra . ē . dim' car̄ . q̄ ibi . ē cū . IIII bord . 7 III . ac̄ pti . 7 VII . q̄z pasturæ lin̄g . 7 III . q̄z in lat̄ . Valet . x . sol.

Robt' ten' de ead *Herpere* . Aluuard tenuit T.R.E. 7 geldb p . III . hid . Tra . ē . III . car̄ . In dn̄io . ē . I . car̄ 7 dimd . 7 III . ferui . 7 II . cofcez . Ibi molin̄ redd. xx . denar̄ . 7 IX . ac̄ pti . 7 IIII . q̄z pasturæ . 7 I . q̄z filuæ . 7 un̄ burḡs redd . VIII . denar̄ . Valuit . c . solid. Modo . IIII . lib.

In ead nilla ten' Robt' de ipsa fem' dimid hid . Sau uin' tenuit p Maner' T.R.E . Tra . ē . dim' car̄ . Valet . XII . sol . 7 VI . denar'.

Ipsa ten' *Wilceswde* . Aluuard tenuit T.R.E. 7 geldb p . III . hid 7 dim' . 7 II . partibz uni' v' . Tra . ē . III . arc

Courlandic.

The Lord's Prayer.

Orat. Dom. Amst. p. 84.

Domesday.

In page 50 of this book, I have given a specimen of the Norman character, cut by Cottrell, which was intended for this celebrated national work. The present is an impression from the same types that the folio edition of Domesday was printed with, and is composed from that part relating to the county of Dorset, p. 84-6. This letter was cut by my late friend Joseph Jackson, in a manner more successful than his fellow-labourer: he also engraved a variety of types for the Rolls of Parliament, a work which will ever reflect honor on the good taste of the present reign.

I am indebted to my friend and antiquary, J. Nichols, for enabling me to gratify the curious with this specimen.

Lampoon 1.

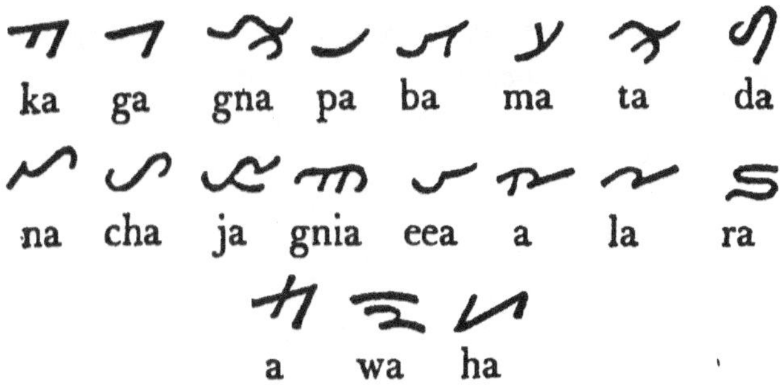

ka ga gna pa ba ma ta da

na cha ja gnia eea a la ra

a wa ha

Lampoon 2.

One	*Sye*	Husband	*Cadjoon*
Two	*Rowah*	Wife	*Cadjoon*
Three	*Tulloo*	Father	*Bapa*
Four	*Ampah*	Mother	*Eenah*
Five	*Leemah*	Head	*Oolooh*
Six	*Annam*	Eyes	*Mattah*
Seven	*Peetoo*	Nose	*Eerong*
Eight	*Ooalloo*	Hair	*Booho*
Nine	*Seewah*	Teeth	*Eepan*
Ten	*Pooloo*	Hand	*Chooloo*
Day	*Rannee*	White	*Mandack*
Night	*Beenghee*	Black	*Malloom*
Good	*Buttie*	Die	*Jahal*
Fire	*Aphooy*	Water	*Wye*
Earth	*Tanno*	Cocoa nut	*Clappah*
Rice	*Beeas*	Fish	*Ewah*
Hog	*Babooye*	Moon	*Boolan*
God	*Alla-talla*	I	*Gniah*

LAMPOON 1.

The alphabet of one of the principal languages spoken in the island of Sumatra.

Marden, p. 168.

LAMPOON 2.

This specimen of the Lampoon tongue, which is spoken in Sumatra, is taken from the Comparative Vocabulary.

Marsden, p. 168.

Monks.

Aa Bb Cc Dd Ee Ff Gg Hh

Ii Kk Ll Mm Nn Oo Pp Qq

Rr Ss Tt Uu Xx Yy Zz

Sclavonian.

а	б	в	г	д	є	ж	ѕ	з
a	b	v	g	d	e	j	z	z
и	ї	к	л	м	н	о	п	р
i	ï	k	l	m	n	o	p	r
с	т	у	ф	х	ц	ч	ш	щ
s	t	u	ph	ch	tz	ch	sch	tsch
ъ	ꙑ	ь	ѣ	є	ю	ѧ	ѳ	ѵ
ier	ieri	ieer	iat	é	yu	ya	th	isch

Rejang 1.

ka	ga	nga	ta	da	na	pa	ba	
ma	cha	ja	nia	sa	ra	la	eea	
ooa	hha	mba	ngga	nda	nja	a		

MONKS.

This alphabet was copied from the original paper, which was sent to the late Edward Cave, and is inserted in the Gentleman's Magazine for 1753, p. 170; which paper was given to me by my friend J. Nichols, F. A. S. the present proprietor of that valuable publication.

The alphabet is called *Novissimæ Monachales*.

SCLAVONIAN.

Or ancient Russian; taken from the Encyc. Franc. pl. X. It was omitted by accident from it's proper place in the work.

REJANG 1.

Another alphabet of one of the principal internal languages used in the island of Sumatra. Of the two figures at the end of the alphabet, the first is the mark of commencement, and the latter of pause.

Marsden, p. 168.

Rejang 2.

One	*Do*	Husband	*Lackye*
Two	*Dooy*	Wife	*Sooma*
Three	*Tellou*	Father	*Bapa*
Four	*'Mpat*	Mother	*Indo*
Five	*Lemo*	Head	*Oolou*
Six	*Noom*	Eyes	*Matty*
Seven	*Toojooa*	Nose	*Eeoong*
Eight	*Delapoon*	Hair	*Boo*
Nine	*Sembilan*	Teeth	*Aypen*
Ten	*Depooloo*	Hand	*Tangoon*
White	*Pooteah*	Black	*Meloo*

Rejang 2.

The above is a specimen of the Rejang language, which is spoken in the island of Sumatra, and is taken from the Vocabulary.

Marsden, p. 168.

www.ingramcontent.com/pod-product-compliance
Lightning Source LLC
Chambersburg PA
CBHW051124120726
47905CB00005B/1411

* 9 7 8 3 7 4 4 7 1 5 2 5 6 *